Karen Horney

Pioneer of Feminine Psychology

Women in Medicine

Karen Horney
Pioneer of Feminine Psychology

Mathilde Krim and the Story of AIDS

Elisabeth Kübler-Ross
Encountering Death and Dying

Rita Levi-Montalcini
Nobel Prize Winner

Mary Eliza Mahoney
and the Legacy of African-American Nurses

Margaret Sanger
Rebel for Women's Rights

WOMEN in MEDICINE

Karen Horney

Pioneer of Feminine Psychology

Susan Tyler Hitchcock

CHELSEA HOUSE
PUBLISHERS
A Haights Cross Communications Company

Philadelphia

COVER: Karen Horney (1885–1952), celebrated psychiatrist and professor, shown here seated with her pet cocker spaniel, Butschi. Karen enjoyed relaxing on summer weekends at her Long Island beach house with her pet and her friends.

CHELSEA HOUSE PUBLISHERS
VP, NEW PRODUCT DEVELOPMENT Sally Cheney
DIRECTOR OF PRODUCTION Kim Shinners
CREATIVE MANAGER Takeshi Takahashi
MANUFACTURING MANAGER Diann Grasse

Staff for KAREN HORNEY
EXECUTIVE EDITOR Lee M. Marcott
PHOTO EDITOR Sarah Bloom
PRODUCTION EDITOR Noelle Nardone
SERIES & COVER DESIGNER Takeshi Takahashi
LAYOUT 21st Century Publishing and Communications, Inc.

A Haights Cross Communications ✦ Company

http://www.chelseahouse.com

First Printing

9 8 7 6 5 4 3 2 1

Library of Congress Cataloging-in-Publication Data

Hitchcock, Susan Tyler.
    Karen Horney : pioneer of feminine psychology / Susan Tyler Hitchcock.
        p. cm.—(Women in medicine)
Includes bibliographical references and index.
    ISBN 0-7910-8025-0
    1. Horney, Karen, 1885-1952. 2. Psychoanalysts—United States—Biography.
I. Title. II. Series.
RC438.6.H67H55 2004
150.19'5'092—dc22
                                                        2004009322

All links and web addresses were checked and verified to be correct at the time of publication. Because of the dynamic nature of the web, some addresses and links may have changed since publication and may no longer be valid.

Table of Contents

The Cost of
Having New Ideas

1

REASONS FOR PRIDE

Psychoanalyst Karen Horney [pronounced HOR-nigh] had every reason to feel proud as she entered the auditorium of the New York Psychoanalytic Society on October 17, 1939. She had made it far along on the path of her choosing. It had not been a likely course to be taken by a woman born in a little German village in 1885. She had had to argue with her parents to let her attend the **Gymnasium**—the German high school—because in those days, few girls continued their education. She had gone from there through medical school into the new field of **psychiatry**. She had steeped herself in the revolutionary ideas of **psychoanalysis**, inspired primarily by the great Viennese doctor, Sigmund Freud. Gaining her credentials, she had earned a position of honor in the Berlin Psychoanalytic Society. There, she had earned a reputation for her intelligence, her originality, and her effectiveness as a therapist, and in 1932 she had received an invitation to travel to the United States and join the newly founded Chicago Psychoanalytic Institute. While no one's life is without its problems, Karen Horney's career so far seemed charmed. From Chicago, she had moved up even further, accepting membership in the New York Psychoanalytic Society and poised to teach classes in its Institute. In New York, she had swiftly found colleagues, students, patients, and friends. She had moved gracefully into the inner circle of the most prestigious organization of psychiatrists in the most sophisticated city in America.

And now, in 1939, she had published her second book. Her first, *The Neurotic Personality of Our Time,* had come out in 1937. In it, Karen Horney had proposed that not just early childhood experiences but also later social and cultural influences shaped an individual's personality. Since then, Horney had become more confident and articulate about her ideas, particularly the concerns she had with some of Freud's basic ideas about human **psychology**. Working closely with her editor, William Warder Norton, who was enthusiastic about her work, she had shaped her next book into something that would be interesting to the general public and yet also useful for the practicing **psychoanalyst**. She had considered several titles—*Open Questions in Psychoanalysis, A Personal Outlook on Psychoanalysis, New Goals in Psychoanalysis*—but she and Norton had settled on *New Ways in Psychoanalysis*. She wanted the title, and the book, to grant all that the field owed to its founder, Sigmund Freud, but she also wanted to question some of Freud's theories.

She had carefully constructed her book. She began by acknowledging the overwhelming importance of Sigmund Freud's work. In her first chapter, she wrote that "the most fundamental and most significant of Freud's findings" was his revolutionary idea that "actions and feelings may be determined by unconscious motivations."[1] All of psychotherapy depended on this basic discovery of Freud's, that memories, feelings, and desires from deep within, often formed early in childhood and never even recognized by a person, can lie behind the decisions and behavior of everyday life. Every therapist was dedicated to helping patients through a long process of discovery. The process involved **analysis**, or recognizing those unconscious motivations, and **therapy**, or reorganizing feelings and behavior based on new understanding.

In her first chapter as well, Karen Horney thanked Freud for the fundamental idea that **psychic** processes are real and therefore as subject to scientific inquiry as physical processes. This new idea, she wrote, allowed therapists and patients to take seriously those "psychic manifestations which had hitherto been regarded as incidental, meaningless or mysterious, such as dreams, fantasies, errors of everyday life."[2] Freud established that childhood experiences have direct links to adult problems. Often the seemingly meaningless, oddball fictions that come out of a person's imagination—the strange occurrences in dreams, the wishes he imagines that could never come true, the times he says one thing but means something quite different—

even these are full of meaning. Often such slips can lead more directly to the unconscious forces of behavior than the actions and statements a person more willingly controls.

To get at the motivations hidden within a person's unconscious, Freud proposed the basic technique of **free association**. Encouraging a patient to talk freely, to let words and ideas flow without reflection or self-control, the therapist helped uncover what was hidden within. Freud also promoted **hypnosis**, a technique that induced a sleeplike state, as a way to reach a new insights and self-awareness. Another essential technique for therapy explained by Freud was **transference**, which meant encouraging the patient to play out and then explore his troubled personal relationships by mirroring them in his interactions with the therapist. Freud had made "pioneering observations" such as these, Horney wrote in her first chapter, and those ideas formed "the mental background" of her entire book.[3]

TAKING ISSUE WITH FREUD

But Horney's colleagues in the Freudian psychoanalytic establishment did not hear her praise of Freud as clearly as they heard her criticism of him. Although grounded in Freud's ideas, New Ways in Psychoanalysis was a point-by-point critique of his theories. Many more words on its pages argued against Freud than praised him. "Psychoanalysis has to rid itself of the heritage of the past if its great potentialities are to develop," Karen Horney dared to write, [4] as she proceeded, chapter by chapter, to take on many of the ideas considered central to the profession. At heart, she took issue with Freud's belief that all adult psychological problems were directly caused by things that happened in infancy and, further, that most of those early life experiences stemmed from the infant's sexual attachments to the mother.

For Freud, every infant, female or male, began by feeling intense sexual satisfaction through physical contact with her or his mother. Every feeling of sexual longing was a repetition of that early experience of intimate contact. Adult sexuality developed through a process of learning. By adolescence, the individual learned to shift desire to new and more appropriate objects of love—in the case of the girl, from mother to father to male peer; in the case of the boy, from mother to female peer. All sorts of jealousies could emerge along the way: the jealousy of a boy toward his father, for example, who is his own mother's rightful sexual partner. If sexual maturation did not evolve as it should, a man could be unduly influenced by what Freud called the **Oedipus complex**: a man's inappropriately strong attachment to his own mother. He named the condition after the Greek tragedy of Oedipus, in which a man who had been orphaned early on unknowingly marries his own mother. Freud proposed that all disturbed adult behavior could be traced back to interruptions, complications, or misalignments that went on during the process of maturing from infantile desire for the mother to adult desire for a fellow adult.

Karen Horney wanted to broaden the picture. For her, many kinds of interactions throughout the course of one's life—in infancy, childhood, adolescence, and adulthood; with parents, siblings, friends, and fellow workers—influenced personality and behavior. A therapist would do better to study the patterns present in an adult patient's personality, to note how that person behaves in the present day and responds to social situations, than to put all the energy and focus on things that happened during his or her infancy. Horney did not question that childhood experiences were formative. She did believe, though, that therapy worked better if the focus was on the present.

"I differ from Freud in that, after recognition of the neurotic trends, while he primarily investigates their genesis I primarily investigate their actual functions and their consequences," Horney stated. Both Freud and Horney were trying to loosen the grip of **neuroses**, or psychological abnormalities, on their patients, but she questioned whether Freud's approach had that sort of practical effect. "Freud believes that by recognizing the infantile nature of his trends the patient will automatically realize that they do not fit into his adult personality and will therefore be able to master them," she wrote. [5]

It was an argument of ideas, but it had repercussions within the young field of psychotherapy. Sigmund Freud had laid the groundwork for an entire profession. His ideas were taken by many as laws of human development and behavior, his techniques as the rules that every practicing psychotherapist must follow. A word had even sprung up to distinguish Freudian psychiatry from any other: psychoanalysis. Only those people who held to Freud's ideas, trained with Freud or one of his followers, and underwent an intense series of meetings with one of those carefully trained Freudians to analyze their own personalities earned the right to call themselves psychoanalysts. Schools connected with groups like the Berlin and Chicago Psychoanalytic Societies, like the Chicago Psychoanalytic Institute, were establishing a required sequence of training that a **psychiatrist**, already holding a medical degree, must follow to call himself or, much more rarely, herself a psychoanalyst.

When Karen Horney put her own doubts about Freud's theories into print, she was risking repercussions throughout this new world of psychoanalysis. She was taking a bold stance, so early in the history of a discipline, yet she had begun to meet failures in her own work with patients and wanted to share alternative techniques that worked for her. When therapy based on Freud's ideas fails, she wrote, a psychoanalyst can only say that such deeply held instincts simply would not change. Horney believed that a broader form of therapy could help every person. "I believe that all the obstacles which Freud holds responsible for therapeutic failures . . . are really due to the erroneous premises on which his therapy is built," she wrote. [6]

By following her proposed "new ways in psychoanalysis," therapists could more reliably succeed in what they all were trying to do—help the patient "to regain his spontaneity, to find his measurements of value in himself, in short, to give him the courage to be himself." [7]

A MEMBER OF THE SOCIETY

Despite her doubts, Karen Horney had eagerly joined ranks with the New York Psychoanalytic Society and actively participated in its meetings. Each month, the members gathered to hear colleagues present papers, analyze cases, and discuss issues of psychoanalytic theory. She valued the forum for discussion and debate. In 1939, though, she and others were sensing more tension in the air. Lawrence Kubie, a 43-year-old psychiatrist with an M.D. from Johns Hopkins, had recently become president of the Society. Despite his gentlemanly demeanor and diplomatic ways, Kubie had a reputation for laying down strict rules and expecting everyone to follow them. Students on their way to becoming **analysts** at the Institute had formally petitioned Kubie in June 1939 to give them, among other things, access to the Society library and more freedom in choosing their courses. Their petition stated that, although the New York Psychoanalytic Institute was founded on the principles of Freudian analysis, they wanted to learn psychological theories beyond those of Sigmund Freud. They specifically mentioned two favorite teachers: Harry Stack Sullivan and Karen Horney.

Sullivan was a New Yorker, the child of poor Irish immigrant parents who had worked his way through medical school to become a psychiatrist. He considered an individual's psychology to be shaped by human relationships and interactions. Like Horney, he was interested in broadening the psychoanalyst's view of the individual. Both Sullivan and Horney drew students to them with their down-to-earth ways and willingness to entertain new ideas about psychology and the work of therapy.

Dr. Kubie invited the petitioning students to come see him in his apartment and air their grievances. He listened to them patiently and told them he would take all their requests into serious consideration. But then, as the next fall semester began, he announced that students were required to follow even more rigid rules at the Institute. The list of required courses got longer, not shorter, which meant their choices became fewer. Karen Horney was no longer teaching a lecture course, open to all students, but rather an elective, open only to a small number of the most advanced students. Harry Stack Sullivan was not teaching a course at all. The students wrote Kubie another letter of protest, but the rules remained.

The students who knew Karen Horney well and who considered her their favorite teacher flocked to her, complaining about what was happening. She had seen it coming. As early as 1937, her requests to teach a course in new techniques of psychotherapy had been denied by those in charge of the Institute, who told her that students "should first get acquainted with Freud's views." [8] The powers that be in the New York Psychoanalytic Society and Institute had been coming to see her as a fly in the ointment: a renegade, someone who dared to criticize the ideas of the great founder of psychoanalysis—and a woman besides. She had always been an original thinker, and she often rubbed people the wrong way. She was used to standing up for herself. She consoled her students, telling them that even though they were meeting with resistance, she would stand firmly by them. They could come consult with her anytime, even if they were not taking classes from her. After all, the Institute hadn't fired her.

On September 23, 1939, Sigmund Freud died. Now it was up to his followers to carry his theory and practice into the future. Traditionalists at psychoanalytic institutes, both in Europe and in the United States, became all the more vigilant about protecting the sacredness of his ideas. Psychoanalysts were by definition supposed to be sensitive about keeping their emotions from driving their rational decisions, but in the drama of the developing field of psychoanalysis, Freud's death cast a critical thinker like Karen Horney into an even more villainous role.

KAREN HORNEY, CENTER STAGE

Despite his doubts—or perhaps because of his doubts— Lawrence Kubie invited Karen Horney to address the October gathering of the New York Psychoanalytic Society. She felt honored and optimistic about the event. She asked that all those planning to attend read four chapters of her new book. She told Kubie that she looked forward to hearing "opposing points of view of colleagues" and was glad to see Society members, including Kubie himself, "sufficiently open-minded as to deviating viewpoints" and therefore open to hearing her learned critiques of Freudian theory.[9] A colleague later remembered that Horney approached her October lecture with a "very friendly and cooperative" attitude.[10] From all indications, the invitation for her to speak suggested that perhaps the psychoanalytic establishment was now willing to move forward and consider new ideas.

On October 17, 1939, Karen Horney presented a talk to the New York Psychoanalytic Society titled "The Emphasis on Genesis in Freud's Thinking." She may have softened her language somewhat for her audience, but her talk clearly repeated the ideas that she had developed in *New Ways in Psychoanalysis.* She questioned what she called Freud's tendency to "evolutionistic–mechanistic thinking."[11] She attributed both ways of thinking—the tendency to explain biology in terms of the process of evolution and the tendency to see life as **mechanistic**, running like a machine—to the era when Freud developed his central ideas, the late nineteenth century.

Like Charles Darwin, the great evolutionary biologist, Freud understood that "things which exist today have not existed in the same form from the very beginning, but have developed out of previous stages." [12] This basic assumption formed the **evolutionistic** thinking at the foundation of all his theories of human psychology. But Freud's version of these ideas was mechanistic, too, in Horney's view. He implied "that present manifestations not only are conditioned by the past, but contain nothing except the past; nothing really new is created in the process of development; what we see today is only the old in a changed form." [13] Like a machine, the human personality kept on running, just as it had from the first. There were direct, logical, and understandable links between one part and another, and those links remained constant throughout its entire operating cycle. Freud saw the **unconscious**—that repository of ancient memories and feelings that controls motivations without our awareness—as timeless. Every individual was compelled to repeat inborn instinctual responses. Believing this, Freud put extraordinary emphasis on "genesis"—or early beginnings—as the inescapable source for all later personality and behavior.

"There is no doubt whatever that childhood experiences exert a decisive influence on development," stated Karen Horney, "and, as I have said, it is one of Freud's many merits to have seen this in greater detail and with more accuracy than it had been seen before." To this audience in particular, she took care to express her full respect and awareness of all Sigmund Freud had contributed to their field. "The question since Freud," she continued, "is no longer whether there is an influence, but how it operates." [14]

Childhood experiences do indeed "exert a decisive influence on development," and those effects "can be directly traced," she acknowledged. A child who is treated badly early in life will grow up unable to trust others. He or she will carry the burden of feeling mistreated all through life, and no matter what the circumstances, those feelings will shade all others, causing extreme sensitivity to bad treatment. Some adults with such a past will feel they are being badly treated, even when they are not. Others with such a past might unconsciously seek situations that lead them into bad treatment, since it feels familiar. "In this sense of, let us say, anticipating evil rather than good, the old experiences enter directly into adult ones," said Horney. [15]

But, she continued, "the other and more important influence is that the sum total of childhood experiences brings about a certain character structure, or rather, starts its development." Some people's character structures continue developing and changing well into adulthood, even into old age. A girl who hated her mother might well grow into a woman who hates her husband. Freud would interpret that as a cause and effect situation. But Horney would argue that her early feelings for her mother are not the only force in play. There have been many more personal interactions—with siblings, friends, boyfriends before the one she married—that have continued to influence how she feels about herself and her relation to her husband. "That the character has developed as it has is accounted for in part by the relation to the mother, but also by the combination of all other factors influential in childhood." [16] Things that happen in later childhood, adolescence, and adulthood can influence a personality as definitively as the early infantile experience. In short, Karen Horney concluded, an individual's life should be viewed as a lifelong accumulation, a more complex developmental process, and not merely a repetition of feelings and attachments dating from infancy.

THE ESTABLISHMENT REACTS

As Karen Horney finished her presentation, there was a silence in the hall. She looked up hopefully, optimistic that she would be appreciated, or at least that the new ideas she was presenting could inspire healthy debate. Two of Horney's closest colleagues, Abram Kardiner and Clara Thompson, began the discussion. They gently rephrased some of her boldest statements, trying their best to bridge the gap that they sensed between the speaker and her audience.

One by one, others began to join in the discussion. The tension mounted. One respondent's tone turned sharp and bitter. Another echoed his angry claim. Arguments seemed to be turning personal. Accusations were being flung across the room. One person interrupted another, then a louder voice interrupted his. One of the older male Society members stood up, pointed a finger angrily at Karen Horney, and shouted at her, demanding that she give examples to prove her claims. Others cheered him on. No one had said it outright, but everyone knew. Those in the meeting were furious at Karen Horney for daring to criticize the great Sigmund Freud. The tone of the audience's reactions had risen far beyond rational discussion. Rage and hostility thickened the air. Lawrence Kubie, interested in the dynamics but wanting to keep the peace, stood up in the front and, yelling out over the clamor, called the meeting to order. Clearly the ideas presented by Dr. Horney roused great interest, he stated. Considering that many had comments to make, Kubie proposed that the present meeting adjourn but that the November meeting be devoted to further discussion of Dr. Horney's paper.

One month later, the New York Psychoanalytic Society reconvened. This time, Karen Horney did not stand at the podium. She sat in the audience like all the other members of the Society. She listened as Lawrence Kubie moderated a discussion that amounted to an attack not only on her critical comments about Freud but also on her personality, her professionalism, and her reputation as a scientist and a psychoanalyst.

No transcript exists of what went on, so the exact words and phrases used can only be imagined. It had to have been difficult for Horney to stomach. One gets a sense of the vicious accusations and attacks slung her way by reading the letter written by her friend, Abram Kardiner, to Lawrence Kubie, blaming him for not keeping the meeting more fair, compassionate, and controlled:

> You permitted the tone of discussion to go unchallenged; . . . you permitted one member to call another a liar on a matter which you—as chairman—should have been able to settle or verify; you permitted scientific slander to take the place of criticism; you permitted unlimited use of the term "orthodoxy," and allowed unchallenged the political device of analyzing the speaker and discussions by slips of the tongue . . . This is an all time low—and yet you have the illusion that it created the impression of fairness. [17]

At one point, Karen Horney turned to the friend sitting next to her and said, "I don't see why we can't have different opinions and still be friends." [17] Those who knew and loved Karen Horney said that for the first time ever, they saw tears welling up in her eyes.

2 Coming of Age

1885–1909

FIGHTING HER WAY INTO SCHOOL

Karen Clementina Theodora Danielsen was born on September 16, 1885, into a family of seven, although she came to know only two of those seven—her mother and her brother—very well. She loved her mother, named Clothilde Marie, but nicknamed Sonni. Likewise she loved and admired her brother, Berndt, although resentments surfaced every time she realized that as a male born in late nineteenth-century Germany, he led a life filled with greater opportunities than she could have. Karen's father, Berndt Henrik Wackels Danielsen, in his late forties when she was born, had been married before, then widowed. The four children from his first marriage, although significantly older than Berndt and Karen, rudely laid claim to the attentions of their father.

Danielsen captained commercial ocean-going steamships, plying the dangerous waters of the South Atlantic and rounding Cape Horn. His ships carried German cargo, especially the parts needed to build new railroads, to cities developing on the west coast of South and Central America. From those destinations, he would bring raw materials back to Europe, like saltpeter, copper, and tin. Occasionally he would bring Karen an oddball souvenir from those faraway lands, like a llama-fur poncho or a carved buffalo horn. A single journey, there and back, would take six months or more, so Wackels Danielsen was rarely home. When he was, though, he was a stern taskmaster, expecting his wife and children to obey him and live according to strict rules of manners and Christianity.

Like most men of his time, Wackels Danielsen believed that girls should be raised to become wives, mothers, and housekeepers. But his wife and his daughter could not help but notice that the times were changing. They lived in the little village of Eilbek, Germany, just outside Hamburg, a city that sits deep in the mouth of the Elbe River, which flows out into the North Sea. Hamburg was an old sea port and business center of Germany, but a devastating fire had destroyed much of the town in 1842. Hope and energy was building as the twentieth century approached and Hamburg was regaining a place as a new and modern center for German and world commerce. With new wealth and new industry come new ideas.

Traditionally, girls in Germany completed school in the eighth grade. They were not allowed to enroll in the Gymnasium, the German word for the high school that offered classes from ninth grade on and prepared students to enter a university. Most Germans accepted the plan as a good idea, but at the turn of the century, enough were questioning the practice that the rules were beginning to change. Germany's first Gymnasium for girls opened in 1894 in Baden, a small town not far south of Hamburg. Many traditionalists were up in arms. "To instruct boys and girls on the same level, with the same method, with the hope of reaching the same goal, is generally viewed as a psychological and pedagogical monstrosity," wrote one objector in a Hamburg newspaper. He was convinced that equal education for girls would bear "bitter fruit in our community and family life." [19] In 1900, amidst such controversy, Hamburg's Gymnasium began offering classes for girls.

Karen Danielsen sprang at the opportunity. She had always been a talker, a writer, and a thinker. She was clever as a child, and family members loved to tell stories of the ways she could amuse them by her independent ways. She played for hours, making up stories and staging them with her dolls. Her favorite was a little sailor boy with many different outfits, probably brought from foreign countries by her father. At the age of eight, though, she decided that she had more dolls than other children in the village. She set several of her own dolls on the ground outside her house, offering them for any child who would like to adopt them. From early on she read avidly, especially novels about the American West. She and her best friend acted out dramatic scenes from the novels. Karen always wanted to play Winnetou, Chief of the Apaches. She sewed costumes and props to match the stories. After she died, her daughter found one of the Apache flags she had made, carefully stored in a box with other things she treasured from childhood.

School absorbed young Karen Danielsen. "It's great in school," she wrote in her diary at the age of fourteen. "My favorite subjects are religion, history, chemistry, and French. I don't like arithmetic at all and the same goes for gym." [20] She studied hard and won the admiration of all her teachers. As she grew into adolescence, those attachments become all-important to Karen, sometimes amounting to lovesick crushes on her part. On the day after Christmas, 1900, when she was fifteen years old, she wrote a list of her teachers in her diary, commenting on each one. Herr Schulze was "heavenly, i.e., interesting, clever, quiet"; Dr. Dietrich was "quite handsome" and "extremely unfair," but "outside school very jolly and nice"; Fraulein Banning was "angelic, charming, interesting, clever, lovable." [21] Already, as a teenager, Karen Horney was analyzing personalities.

In 1899, when a doctor visited to tend Karen during a bout of flu, she grilled him with questions about the profession of medicine. Her vague childhood interest in going to medical school evolved into an unswerving dedication. By setting that goal for herself, she automatically plotted out a difficult passage of education, at least for a girl in Germany in those days. She had to take a university entrance test, the *Abitur,* to fulfill her goal. To pass the Abitur, she had to attend the Gymnasium. She could travel daily to Hamburg by train. It was just a 32-minute ride. Her plans were set.

When he heard Karen's plans, her father put his foot down. No woman in his family would take such steps against tradition. "I wanted to go right away to the Gymnasium for girls, in my thoughts I was there already, but I had not taken

Father into account," the frustrated young girl wrote in December 1900. "He can forbid me the Gymnasium, but the wish to study he cannot," she declared to her diary. She wrote out a radical plan. Karen Danielsen would not let any authority steer her off-course, least of all her cold, hard father, who was home so little, he barely knew her. Her plan was, as she wrote in her diary, to spend six more months with her mother in Einbelt and pass her Abitur; then six months of study in Paris; a year of study at a teaching school; then "a couple of years as a teacher or tutor and preparing myself for final exams and medicine, on my own." The fifth step in her plan stated her goal unequivocally: "And ultimately: doctor." [22] The plan showed a willingness to break all rules and a confidence that things would always go her way. "Fate will have an easy time with me," believed Karen Danielsen. "I prescribe everything for him." [23]

As it turned out, Karen Danielsen did not need to prescribe her fate. Her father ultimately agreed with her plan to educate herself for medical school. She enrolled in Gymnasium classes in late January 1901. Boarding a train, she was embarking on a new phase of life, seeking her own path and her own self apart from home and family.

FALLING IN LOVE WITH LOVE

Karen Horney began keeping a diary at the age of 13. Four years later, as romance entered her life, its pages filled with poetry, meditations, private ramblings that soared with hope and ecstasy, then plummeted into despair and loneliness. Like most other young women coming of age, Horney was fascinated with the dynamics of falling in love.

First there was Schorschi—probably the young man's last name, but "Schorschi" was all that Karen ever wrote down to identify him. The two seem to have met at the Danielsen home on Christmas Eve in 1903. Karen describes it as if it was a mysterious occurrence over which she had no control, a sort of magical intersection between the man of her private dreams and a young man who happened to walk into her life.

> It came overnight, came creeping like a thief. . . . I was fond of him, that I knew. But that that was love, the dawning of young love's happiness, didn't occur to me. I had indeed yearned madly for love, my whole being dissolved in this one great longing, but it had been purely abstract ecstasy . . . And then on the next day, as he covered my tear-stained face with kisses, as I kissed him, it all seemed a matter of course to me, so natural, as if it had always been so. And the next day . . . was full of dreamlike happiness, I was so blissful, so divinely happy in my half unconscious enjoyment. And he too was happy. [24]

Horney was, she wrote in her diary, "awakened to life," with a "heavenly joy in my heart." [25] "I love you, dear year of 1903," she wrote on New Year's Eve, "because you have given me the highest and the best we human beings can have—love." [26]

"Why don't you write, Schorschi?" Karen Danielsen was writing in her diary not even two weeks later. "Don't you know that my soul is sick with longing for a greeting from you?" [27] What had appeared a transcendent moment of love turned out in retrospect to be a fling of the moment. She poured her sorrows out in poetry.

> Do you love me still? Was it only a jest?
> My heart quivers in a torment of doubt—
> My eyes gaze dim into the distance. [28]

Like so many first loves, the experience was devastating and yet thrilling. Karen Danielsen emerged from this speedy love affair fascinated by the emotional experiences of love and dejection. Soon she had fallen in love again. This time we know the fellow by his first name only—Rudolf, or Rolf for short—

and we know that, despite difficult periods and uncertainties in the minds of both, Rolf and Karen spent a lot of time together for the next full year. He was a struggling musician who could barely make ends meet. His friends were young intellectuals, full of questions about art and philosophy, and Karen fit right into their lengthy conversations. Rolf was Jewish, which made no difference to Karen Danielsen, but it did concern her older brother and her mother. Neither his class nor his religion, they believed, would make him the right husband for Karen.

After Rolf, there was Ernst. She recorded a day in Berlin together. "Wine parlors, the first big binge of my life—taxi-cab—. . . my old ardent love for Ernst flamed up again in all its terrible glory. A few hours—no, days—a nameless, blissful, engulfing happiness, then it was all over." [29] Through each romance, Karen Danielsen was sharpening her young woman's understanding of human behavior. She observed, analyzed, and wrote in her diary the twists and turns of emotion that she sensed in herself, the responses that she saw in others and the meanings that she thought they might hold. She wanted to be loved, but perhaps even more urgently, she wanted to understand what it meant to love and to be in love. "I long for one thing more," she wrote her diary one New Year's Eve: "to learn how to listen to the delicate vibrations of my soul, to be incorruptibly *true to myself* and fair to others, to find in this way the right measure of my own worth." [30]

MRS. OSKAR HORNEY

As Karen Danielsen was exploring relationships with men, the marriage between her parents was disintegrating. Wackels Danielsen's dictatorial personality, months of separation followed every time by an abrupt change in household dynamics, the tensions with his four older children—all drove Sonni Danielsen to decide to separate from her husband in August 1904. She moved into the city of Hamburg with her two children, into a house large enough that they could rent rooms out as a way to make money. "Better to live a poor life with strangers than to go back to slavery and to *this* man," Sonni wrote to her son, revealing a depth of feeling she had not so boldly expressed when her children were younger. "You can look at my stubbornness as obstinacy or sickness— I would rather be dead." [31] For Berndt and Karen, then aged 21 and 19, there was no question: wherever their mother was, that was home for them. They were each, furthermore, approaching the age when they would be making homes of their own.

In the spring of 1906, Karen Danielsen passed the *Abitur*, the test allowing her entry into a university. Restrictions for women in German education existed at the university level as well in those days. Few German universities admitted women as regular students working toward a college degree. Women could visit classes, but they could not enroll. But the University of Freiburg had made the first moves to change this policy and had recently granted its first degree to a woman. This news made Karen Danielsen choose to attend the university in Freiburg, and she moved there, planning to spend the next two years studying medicine. Considering the situation, it was unlikely there would be many, if any, other women studying medicine with her, but in some ways that situation appealed to Danielsen.

Freiburg was an old city in the far southwest of Germany, close to France and Switzerland, nearly 500 miles away from Hamburg, a twelve-hour train ride. It presented a different landscape altogether, set as it was in the Black Forest, with gorgeous hillside scenery all around. The city was different, too—compared to the bustling seaport of Hamburg, Freiburg was an antique town, with centuries-old buildings, little cobbled streets, and a magnificent Gothic cathedral soaring over all.

On a July evening in this picturesque town, Danielsen joined other students in an annual celebration. The party went on into the night, and Karen found herself in the company of two young men, also university students: Louis Grote and Oskar Horney.

> We [she and Louis Grote] danced a Française together . . . we threw rose-leaves at each other on the veranda, which was decorated with colored lanterns . . . we went arm-in-arm down the Schlossberg at three in the morning and out to the suburb of Guntherstal. And suddenly somebody was walking beside us, telling one story after another—it was the little Hornvieh [her nickname for Horney]. Somewhat later we sat on Hornvieh's balcony, dangling our legs and laughing at each other, happy and surprised, not understanding our being together there at all. And then it was all the way up the steep road to the Solacker hill in dancing slippers and ball dress. Up there we lay in the sun and gradually our eyes fell gently shut. [32]

It was the start of a threeway friendship that would last a long time. At first, Karen fell for "Losch," as she called Louis Grote. Over time, though, her affections grew for "the Hornvieh," as she called Oskar Horney—a nickname for his last name, but also a tease, since the same word could mean "blockhead" in German. These three freewheeling students, Danielsen, Grote, and Horney, became inseparable. At first, Karen felt herself especially close to Louis Grote. But when Oskar Horney left Freiburg a year later, she missed him tremendously. In fact, she stopped writing in her diary and began writing long letters to him instead.

Soon after Karen moved to Freiburg, Sonni Danielsen decided to move there, too. In part, she was worried about her daughter. One of the only women amidst hundreds of young men, Karen seemed to have little regard for the rules of society. She went out drinking, took long mountain hikes, made friends more often with men than with women. Mrs. Danielsen did not want her daughter to earn the reputation of being an immoral woman—or, worse yet, to find herself pregnant and unmarried. To support herself, Sonni Danielsen once again opened a boardinghouse. Karen moved back in with her mother. She felt delighted, not restricted, by their closeness. Home was now, she wrote Oskar Horney, "inexpressibly cozy," thanks to the way her mother could "spread about her a fluid atmosphere" and cook well, too. She thought back on her childhood home of Hamburg, so far away, and realized it no longer felt like home to her. "In Hamburg there is only my father," Karen wrote, "and I have no contact with him." [33]

Karen Danielsen finished medical school in 1908. Before actually beginning to practice medicine, she was required to apprentice as a **medical resident**. She moved to another university town, Göttingen in central Germany, to do so. Her choice probably had a lot to do with Oskar Horney: his parents lived very close to Gottingen, and she knew he would be able to visit her there. In less than a year, the two had decided to marry. No longer writing a diary, Karen Danielsen never wrote down her personality analysis of this man she had chosen to be her husband. She kept her reasons for choosing him to herself, but they seemed clear to those who knew her. He had been a loyal friend for years. He had listened to her, staying steady through many of her emotional ups and downs. Even through times when she thought she was falling in love with other men, and told Oskar Horney so, he stayed loyal to her. He seemed not just tolerant but even appreciative of Karen's professional accomplishments and future ambition, and that was a character trait hard to find in German men in those days. Furthermore, his future looked bright, too. Having received a Ph.D. in political science at the University of Freiburg, Oskar Horney had accepted a job with the Stinnes Corporation, a successful coal and power company. In October 1909, Karen and Oskar Horney were married in Berlin, the lively capital city of Germany, where they embarked on a new life together.

Rebellious Wife, Rebellious Psychiatrist

1909–1927

3

WIFE AND THERAPIST

At first, Karen and Oskar Horney lived a charmed life. Oskar moved quickly up the ranks in his business. The Stinnes Corporation grew richer and more powerful, buying up property and businesses throughout Germany and Eastern Europe. By 1920, the corporation had become a major industrial presence in Europe. As Oskar's position and salary increased, he and Karen moved into a house in a fashionable suburb of Berlin. Their first child, Brigitte, was born in 1911; Marianne was born in 1913; and Renate, the youngest of their three daughters, was born in 1916. There were family losses as well—Karen's father died in 1910, and less than a year later, her mother died as well. Karen Horney genuinely missed her mother's warmth and spirit, but her death also represented a release from parental obligations at a time when the demands in her own household were growing.

Karen Horney was never just a housewife, however. As Oskar's job developed, she immersed herself in her own medical studies. She decided to specialize in the field of psychiatry—the diagnosis and treatment of mental and psychological illnesses. At the start of the twentieth century, psychiatry was a relatively new field of medicine. Doctors specializing in the new field held to the view that psychiatry, as much as any sort of internal medicine, was a physical science. A psychiatrist was particularly interested in discovering the reasons for pains and diseases that could not be easily tracked back to physical causes. Nearly all of Horney's professors, though, scoffed at the new theories of Sigmund Freud, the Viennese doctor who was proposing psychological causes for these discomforts. Freud diagnosed his patients by using unorthodox methods such as hypnosis, dream interpretation, and free-ranging associations between ideas, which he encouraged his patients to make and talk about. (For more information on hypnosis, enter "hypnosis and psychotherapy" into any

Sigmund Freud and the Birth of Psychotherapy

Sigmund Freud was born in Moravia in 1856 but lived from childhood until the last year of his life in Vienna, Austria. He studied medicine and established a private practice treating psychological disorders, his specialty. In his first published study, he discussed what was then called "hysteria"—the experience of physical symptoms without any physical cause.

One famous patient of his, called Anna O. in his writings, experienced all sorts of unexplainable problems ranging from paralysis and tunnel vision to fantasies and attempted suicide. For a while, she refused to drink any water. While under hypnosis, Anna O. revealed that she had once seen a woman drink water from the same glass that a dog had just drunk from. It so upset her that she stopped drinking water herself. Her case led Freud to articulate one of his basic ideas: Unexpressed responses to traumatic past events often lie behind abnormal present-day behavior. When Anna O. remembered the scene of the woman drinking from the dog's glass, she was willing to start drinking water again. This step led Freud to recognize another basic idea of human psychology: Remembering and articulating past traumas can release their grip on a person's mind and behavior.

These revelations form the basis of the modern science of psychiatry and the modern practice of psychotherapy, both originating in the work of Sigmund Freud. Freud soon learned in his own work with patients that hypnosis was not necessary to bring deep memories out in patients. Often he would just have them lie on a couch comfortably in his office and talk freely. Dr. Freud would listen carefully, noting the associations they made and trying to interpret them in light of other things he knew about the patient's personality and past. These unusual sessions between doctor and patient, which took place in the early years of the twentieth century in Vienna, are the prototype for all psychotherapy sessions going on by the millions around the world today.

search engine and browse the sites listed.) To many of Karen Danielsen's psychiatry professors at Berlin's medical school, Freud's ideas were hocus pocus.

It was this new line of psychiatric exploration, however, that Karen Horney found most intriguing. She kept her fascination quiet, pursuing traditional studies during the day then spending the evening hours learning about the Freudian approach, which many were calling "dynamic psychiatry" as well as "psychoanalysis." She attended lectures and avidly read articles and books, not only by Freud himself but also by Carl Jung, Otto Rank, and Alfred Adler. She also embarked on an intense round of psychoanalysis with Karl Abraham, the only German psychiatrist of the day who paid Freud any credence. Horney visited Abraham's office five or six times a week. During the appointment, she would be seated in a place where she could not see Dr. Abraham, to encourage her to let her thoughts roam free, her words come out unrestricted by any concern for who was listening. Sometimes she would focus on a dream, telling its story then exploring the associations it raised in her mind. At the end of the session, Dr. Abraham sometimes took a few minutes to discuss his interpretations. She listened to learn about psychotherapy, but she also listened to learn about herself.

It was a lot for Karen Horney to juggle: wife, mother, and on her way to becoming an M.D. and psychoanalyst, too. She enjoyed an active social life, sometimes entertaining at home with her husband and at other times going out with the friends she was making in psychoanalytical circles. Her emotions would ride high, then she would plummet into despair. Her unhappiness felt like a "dreadful fatigue" and she sometimes plunged into "spasms of sobbing."[34] Exploring her emotions through psychoanalysis with Dr. Abraham brought her some relief. Writing in her diary helped her understand herself even more.

Other Disagreements with Freud

Karen Horney was not the only psychologist who dared to differ with the basic theories of Sigmund Freud. Three of the earliest to take issue with Freud were Carl Jung, Otto Rank, and Alfred Adler.

Carl Jung, a Swiss psychiatrist born in 1875, proposed that the unconscious is made up of two layers. One, as Freud proposed, was highly personal, made of impressions from the lifetime of the individual. The other, Jung suggested, was shared by all members of the human race. He called it the "collective unconscious" and suggested that from it arise the stories and symbols that make up our dreams, art, and religion.

Otto Rank, born in 1884, worked as Sigmund Freud's close friend and aide in Vienna for twenty years. His first interest was the application of psychology to myths, but unlike Jung, he did not believe in a collective unconscious. He believed that the trauma of birth affected everyone's psyche, which was a departure from Freud's emphasis on the formative relationship of infant to mother after birth. Rank wanted psychotherapy to last months, not years, which was another point of disagreement between him and his mentor, Freud.

Alfred Adler, born in Vienna in 1870, had already written a book on the health problems of tailors when he was invited by Sigmund Freud to join his circle and explore the new science of psychology. Adler never agreed with Freud that sexual issues stand at the core of human problems. Four years later he left Freud's circle and formed his own school of psychology, based on the idea that people's personalities develop as they build up defenses to protect their own actual or imagined deficiencies. While Adlerian psychology is still respected, it never built a following as did Freudian.

THE HORNEY HOUSEHOLD

With such a busy routine, Karen Horney hired other women to care for her children, first nannies when they were young and then governesses when it was time for them to begin more formal learning. She set the tone for child-rearing in the household, though, making sure that her three daughters grew up in an atmosphere of fresh air, freedom of expression, and tolerance for all sorts of behaviors that other mothers might not have allowed. She was fascinated—and took notes, in fact—when her daughters put their dolls between their legs and pretended they were giving birth to their own babies. She allowed her children extremes of independence not ordinarily offered. When Brigitte contracted tuberculosis at the age of six, her mother sent her to a treatment center in the Swiss Alps all by herself. Soon worried over how deeply her second child missed her older sister, Horney sent five-year-old Marianne off to the same treatment center, even though she was not ill. Marianne Horney later remembered feeling terrified during those days of separation from home and parents. [35]

Things began to fall apart in the Horney household in the early 1920s. There were personal reasons. Karen found it hard to stay faithful to her husband. As Karen lost interest in their intimate relationship, Oskar found female companionship elsewhere, too. Their work, their friends, their interests took them in different directions. Their politics put them at odds: Oskar Horney was a conservative, while Karen Horney supported the socialist movement. They may well have had arguments on how to raise their children, for Karen Horney was determined that her three daughters would grow up to be strong, independent, and opinionated women.

It was an economic blow that struck the Horney household the hardest, though. The German economy had been struggling since the end of World War I. Across the country, Germans felt the effects of inflation—an economic trend when money falls in value, so things cost more and more. German marks lost value so quickly, you might pay one price in the morning and a significantly higher one in the afternoon. Amidst this difficult economic period, the owner of the Stinnes Corporation died. Soon the company collapsed. Oskar Horney lost his job swiftly and unexpectedly. A bout with meningitis damaged his health and perhaps his mental faculties, and from 1923 on, he found his fortune and his future dwindling. By 1926, Oskar Horney was bankrupt.

Within the next year, Karen Horney decided to separate from her husband. In a move that parallelled that of her mother twenty-two years before, she and her three daughters, now aged 15, 13, and 10, moved into an apartment. They even rented out one room to bring in extra money. Unlike Sonni Danielsen, though, Karen Horney had a profession—and during the next six years her career as a psychoanalyst would blossom.

BECOMING A PROFESSIONAL

In the same way that Karen Horney chose an unorthodox approach to being a wife and mother, she did so as a psychiatrist as well. She began working at a private psychiatric hospital in Berlin, treating patients from 1912 on. She studied and practiced the theories of psychoanalysis. Knowing that she had to jump official hurdles in order to get her medical degree, she wrote her dissertation, "A Case Report on the Question of Traumatic Psychosis," on a man whose psychological problems could be traced back to a blow on the head—a subject that fit right into the traditional definition of medical psychiatry and had little to do with Freudian psychoanalysis.

But once she had received her medical degree, Horney clearly declared herself a member of the Freudian camp. She delivered a lecture in 1917 titled "The Technique of Psychoanalytic Therapy," which contrasted medical psychiatrists, who focus on the symptoms, with psychoanalysts, who look into the origins of those symptoms instead. "We may compare psychoanalysis with the excavation of a buried city, in which we assume the existence of valuable historical documents," she explained. [36] As the hidden history gets revealed through talk and interactions between

Freud's Words for the Human Psyche

Just as a surgeon uses words to name the body parts on which he is operating, so a psychologist needs to name the parts at work inside a person's thoughts and feelings. Sigmund Freud proposed a basic vocabulary of psychology that has become part of our everyday language.

Freud came to understand that unacknowledged feelings or memories can still exert a strong force on personality, behavior, and decisions. To name that repository of still-active, although unrecognized, forces in the human psyche, he provided the word "unconscious." For example, a boy was badly bitten by a dachshund at the age of three. At the age of 25, he does not remember the incident at all. But one day, while he is lounging at a friend's house, a dachshund runs up and jumps onto his lap. He jumps up, terrified, and shoves the dog violently. Everyone else wonders why he had such an extreme reaction. Freud would say that he had an abnormal fear of dachshunds in his unconscious.

Freud also proposed that we consider a person's psychological being as divided into three parts: the id, the ego, and the superego. The id,—Latin for "it," is the most primitive part of an individual, the urges and needs at the core of being. The ego,—Latin for "I," is the central sense of self, the conscious self-image a person carries, and the part of the person that mediates among id, the superego, and the outside world. The superego, Latin for "above the ego," can be seen as a person's conscience, aware of laws, rules, and other people's expectations. These three parts of a personality often have conflicting urges, and every human decision requires a balance between all three.

patient and therapist, the abnormal symptoms lessen, according to Freudian theory.

"How does the physician obtain knowledge of the unconscious?" she asked rhetorically in her lecture. Through free association: the psychoanalytic patient should be encouraged to say "everything that occurs to him, no matter whether he considers it trite, ridiculous, absurd, indiscreet or, most important, whether it might be embarrassing to him." Amid these ramblings, the patient may reveal unconscious instincts that had before been locked up "like strange animals"—antisocial desires like a young boy's wanting to kill his father or a young girl's yearning to be a boy instead. Once those instincts are voiced and acknowledged, the patient can "affirm them, reject them or sublimate them," by which she meant use their energy for more productive ends. [36] The lecture ended on a cautious but positive note. "Psychoanalysis can free a human being who has been tied hands and feet. It cannot give him new arms or legs," Horney stated. "Psychoanalysis, however, has shown us that much that we have regarded as constitutional merely represents a blockage of growth, a blockage which can be lifted." [38]

All the while she was studying and treating patients with psychoanalysis, Karen Horney was experiencing it as a patient as well. As a therapy patient, Horney worked with Dr. Abraham for an intense but relatively short period of time, about a year and a half. With him, she certainly experienced "transference," the hallmark of the Freudian psychoanalytic process by which the very difficulties a patient experiences in close personal relationships start coloring the relationship with the therapist, too. The patient transfers problems over to the analyst, providing a vivid, present-day example of his or her personality. Horney's connection with Karl Abraham was complex: he was doctor and colleague, father figure and intruder into her private life. Berlin's psychoanalytically inclined practitioners, including Horney, had begun to coalesce into a social group, centering in large part on Abraham, who hosted weekly evening discussions. This group also formed the core membership of the Berlin Psychoanalytic Institute, rising to importance within the profession during the 1920s.

A POSITION OF INFLUENCE

The Berlin Institute was at once a professional society, a school, a research institute, a clinic, and a meeting place for likeminded intellectuals. Its members tended toward socialist or even Marxist political views. Its free clinic provided psychoanalysis to any citizen free of charge. Sigmund Freud himself applauded the Berlin Institute for making "our therapy accessible to the great numbers of people who suffer no less than the rich from neurosis, but are not in a position to pay for treatment." [39]

Karen Horney was the only woman among the Institute's six founders and the first woman to teach classes there. Her classes included regular case seminars, in which she would discuss in detail a therapeutic patient's symptoms, diagnosis, and treatment, using them as examples to teach how psychoanalysis works. She taught a course in sexual biology to students without prior medical training. She offered lectures, which drew people not only from among the Institute's inner circle but from Berlin's larger intellectual community. She served on the influential education committee, which designed the training program at the Institute. Essentially, students had to fulfill three requirements: undergo personal psychoanalysis, complete a series of courses, and provide psychoanalysis to several patients under the guidance of a mentor. Ultimately these basic rules, written for the Berlin Institute with significant input from Karen Horney, were adopted throughout the world as the guidelines for training psychoanalysts.

Her students grew to love her. She treated them more like friends than did many of her male colleagues. She often invited students to her home and even continued analysis with them when she was on vacation. One of her students was Fritz Perls, who later developed **Gestalt therapy**, an analysis technique focusing on the present rather than the past. (For more information on this technique, enter "gestalt therapy" into any search engine and browse the sites listed.) One teacher just left him confused, another made him felt inferior, but from Karen Horney, he recalled years later, he got "human involvement without terminology." [40] Another student recalled that "she had a certain talent for really understanding people much better than many other analysts." What's more, he said, she was "rather nice to all of us. She had a Ping-Pong table in her apartment and played Ping-Pong with us. I don't think many teachers would have done that." [41] The loyalty she inspired in her students would become important to Karen Horney as the years went by. She did not always evoke such deep devotion among her colleagues.

Firmly grounded in the Berlin psychoanalytic establishment, Horney began to take issue with fellow analysts' ideas, especially their ideas about the psychology of women. The first hint that she would break with Freud and his followers on this subject came in 1922, when she presented a paper at an international meeting of psychoanalysts. Her topic was the "**castration complex**" in women, an idea expressed especially by Freud and Abraham. They believed that every little girl, once she sees a boy or man with a penis, begins to fear that she once had a penis, too, but had lost it. This complex, or cluster of feelings, is caused in girls "by the sight of the genitals of the other sex," Freud wrote. "They at once notice the difference and, it must be admitted, its significance too. They feel seriously wronged, often declare that they want to 'have something like it too,' and fall a victim to 'envy for the penis.'" This experience, which Freud identified as "the discovery that she is castrated," he considered "a turning-point in a girl's growth." [42] Eventually, of course, she learns the biological truth, but the horror that comes with her childhood misconceptions never goes away.

Horney delivered her 1922 lecture "On the Genesis of the Castration Complex in Women" to an esteemed group of psychoanalysts. Freud himself presided over the meeting. Using several actual case studies of her patients, Horney raised the possibility that women's responses to gender differences are not quite what Freud suggested. She tread lightly, however, never outright rejecting the ideas of **penis envy** or the castration complex, but subtly asking whether these ideas truly fit reality. "The conclusion so far drawn from the investigations," she suggested coyly, amounts to "an assertion that one half of the human race is discontented with the sex assigned to it." [43] She let that statement stand without carrying the argument any further. In 1922, Karen Horney was not quite ready to tackle the Freudian establishment.

Four years later, she was.

A MALE GENIUS'S CREATION

Sigmund Freud celebrated his seventieth birthday on May 5, 1926. As is common in academic circles, several of his devoted friends and students decided to invite leading psychoanalysts to write chapters for a *Festschrift,* a book in his honor. Karen Horney contributed an essay titled "The Flight from Womanhood." She told a friend that she considered it like a stone wrapped inside cotton batting—hard-hitting, nearly a weapon, yet couched in the soft and subtle language of praise and compliments.

"Psychoanalysis is the creation of a male genius, and almost all those who have developed [Freud's] ideas have been men," she begins. "It is only right and reasonable that they should evolve more easily a masculine psychology and understand more of the development of men than of women." [44] After repeating the basic Freudian concepts about a girl's psychology, Horney asserts that "science has often found it fruitful to look at long-familiar facts from a fresh point of view"—and for the rest of her article, she does. [45] Female psychology has been constructed thus far "under the spell" of a male point of view, and "if we try to free our minds from this masculine mode of thought, nearly all the problems of feminine psychology take on a different appearance." [46] The female body, with its capacity for giving birth and nurturing a child, gives a woman "by no means negligible physiological superiority," and in fact boys often show "an intense envy of motherhood." [47] Horney suggested that perhaps women feel envy toward the social privileges given to men much more than they envy the parts of a male body. "In actual fact a girl is exposed from birth onward to the suggestion . . . of her inferiority" and the "actual social subordination of women," she pointed out. [48]

Karen Horney recognized that her argument could topple certain fundamental ideas of Freud's psychology. She concluded with a careful, rational, and direct statement, hoping to couch her ideas in language to which all could agree.

> In the foregoing discussion I have put a construction upon certain problems of feminine psychology, which in many points differs from current views. It is possible and even probable that the picture I have drawn is one-sided from the opposite point of view. But my primary intention in this paper was to indicate a possible source of error arising out of the sex of the observer, and by so doing to make a step forward toward the goal that we are all striving to reach: to get beyond the subjectivity of the masculine or the feminine standpoint and to obtain a picture of the mental development of woman that will be more true to the facts of her nature—with its specific qualities and its differences from that of man—than any we have hitherto achieved. [49]

Few of her colleagues responded immediately to Horney's daring attack on established ideas. Freud himself did not comment publicly until five years later, when he referred to Horney in an article on "Female Sexuality." In response to her claim that psychoanalysts overestimate the importance of penis envy in girls and women, Freud simply wrote, "This does not agree with the impression that I myself have formed." [50]

While she did not provoke the sort of intellectual discussion that she would have preferred, Karen Horney felt satisfied that she had communicated her ideas and that she had been heard. Criticism had been voiced, but that was to be expected in response to a woman brash enough to take on the psycho-analytic establishment. No one had done anything to question her reputation or jeopardize her career.

Those moves would come later.

Scenes from the Life
of Karen Horney

Karen Danielsen, at age 3 1/2. Born Karen Clementina Theodora Danielsen on September 15, 1885. Karen wanted for nothing—nothing, that is, but the love of her father. A wealthy ship captain, Wackels Danielsen was stern and strict at home but told stories of adventure on the high seas to Karen's willing ears. His gifts from afar were among Karen's most prized possessions. She learned early, though, that her brother would always be her father's favorite.

Karen's mother, Clothilde Marie van Ronzelen Danielsen, also known as "Sonni." Married to Karen's father when she was 28 and he 44, Sonni made the best of life with the domineering, intolerant sea captain, finally leaving him with their two children in August 1904. Sonni always fostered Karen's ambitions, and by all accounts, Karen had a good relationship with her mother.

Karen's father, Berndt Henrik Wackels Danielsen. Danielsen, a Norwegian-born sea captain, met his daughter for the first time at her christening, when she was already two months old. His frequent time away from home didn't bother Karen and her brother, who found him intolerably stern and terrifying. When at home, he would rule with an iron fist. A strict Evangelical Lutheran, Danielsen was even purported to throw the family Bible at the children and their mother upon occasion in fits of pious rage.

Karen and her brother, Berndt, four years her senior. This photo, taken when Karen was 7 and Berndt 11, implied their close relationship. When Karen wanted to attend a college-preparatory high school (called a *Gymnasium* in German), Berndt sided with his mother in supporting his sister's endeavors. Berndt's early death in 1923, at the age of 41, left Karen disconsolate.

Karen and Oskar Horney with daughters Brigitte (standing) and Marianne (on Karen's lap). Third daughter Renate was not yet born. Though apparently doting parents in this photo, in actuality neither Karen nor Oskar had much time for their daughters, who, for the most part, were placed under the care of a governess or were sent away to boarding school.

Karen Horney at 33, playing the piano. By 1918, when this photo was taken, Horney had married Oskar Horney, given birth to three daughters, obtained her medical degree, and was moving toward practicing psychoanalysis more than she was medicine. Meanwhile, her home country of Germany was in a state of unrest at the end of World War I.

Karen Horney's daughters (from left to right): Marianne, Renate, and Brigitte. Brigitte, the oldest, found a lucrative career in German films, whereas Marianne followed in her mother's footsteps, obtaining her medical degree and practicing psychoanalysis. Renate, the youngest, followed a more traditional path as homemaker and mother, eventually escaping Nazi Germany with her husband, to settle in Mexico.

Lawrence Kubie (1896–1973), president of the New York Psychoanalytic Society during Karen Horney's tenure there. Kubie and others at the Institute felt that Horney's book *New Ways in Psychoanalysis* crossed the line in its disagreements with Freudian theory. On April 29, 1941, Kubie presided over a business meeting of the society during which Horney's teaching status was reduced from instructor to lecturer, keeping her from teaching young students "impure theory."

Franz Alexander, a colleague of Karen Horney in Germany, left Berlin to form the Institute for Psychoanalysis in Chicago. In 1931, he invited Karen to join him as assistant director, to help set up the program. Within two years, however, differences in their views on how psychoanalysis should be taught—Alexander was the more conservative—caused Horney to leave America's first psychoanalytic institute. She moved to New York City, where she opened a private practice and lectured at the New York Psychoanalytic Society.

Sigmund Freud, Viennese physician and founder of psychoanalysis, in 1938. Freud suggested that all psychological activity was the result of the interaction of conflicting mental forces and that every infant is born "programmed" to pursue pleasure and to avoid pain. Karen Horney, although trained in Freudian psychoanalysis, began to differ with Freud's theories, especially those concerning women.

Erich Fromm, German social philosopher. Horney met Fromm, as well as other great minds of the period, in a café in Berlin, and he quickly became a member of her inner circle of friends. Fromm used Freudian theory to analyze social problems, whereas Horney took social issues into account when forming psychoanalytic theory. Hence, they developed a strong working and personal relationship that lasted for years.

Karl Menninger, prominent psychologist who with his father William Claire
Menninger founded the Menninger Clinic in Topeka, Kansas. Horney
befriended Menninger upon her arrival in the United States, but Menninger,
a conservative psychoanalyst, later turned against Horney and her followers.

Margaret Mead, world-renowned anthropologist, whose work concerning the influence of culture on human behavior interested Karen Horney. Horney wrote to Mead in 1935, suggesting they meet to discuss issues such as "female 'qualities' and their being subject to cultural factors." Despite their different fields of study, they corresponded with one another. In this 1954 photo, Mead, then Associate Curator of Ethnology at the American Museum of Natural History, holds two examples of Manus Art she brought back from a 7-month visit to the Manus Village in the Admiralty Islands.

Into the Heart
of American
Psychoanalysis

4

1928–1934

LEAVING GERMANY

While Karen Horney was never much interested in politics, the state of affairs in Germany in the late 1920s and early 1930s could not help but unsettle her. When the U.S. stock market crashed in October 1929, a financial crisis rippled through the world. Recovering from the inflationary period that ruined Oskar Horney, Germany had enjoyed a brief period of economic stability and cultural flowering, centered in Berlin. Now, in response to the Wall Street crash, the country plunged into another devastating depression.

As more German men lost their jobs, they looked with resentment on those they believed less deserving of employment, especially women and Jews. A newly elected government, with the Nazi Party in the majority, declared a state of emergency and enforced more stringent social controls. The policies now being announced publicly by such rising leaders as Joseph Goebbels and Adolf Hitler put all German Jews on alert. Anyone with liberal views worried that they, too, might soon lose the comforts and privileges of daily life. Although Karen Horney was not Jewish, many of her friends and colleagues were.

Hitler moved into a position of power within the government in 1933 and became president one year later. Soon political enemies of the Nazis—the socialists and communists—were being arrested and sent to prison. Next Hitler's racial policy of **anti-Semitism** and the superiority of the **Aryan Race**, white and non-Jewish, became law. Nazi police began arresting people simply because they were Jewish.

Many German intellectuals, Jewish or not, found ways to leave their homeland, worried about the Nazi regime. As an Aryan woman, Karen Horney would not have suffered severely, but she had a sense that her social and professional circle could not survive. Her instincts were right. The Nazis considered psychoanalysis a "Jewish science" in large part because Freud and many of his closest followers were Jews. Nazi police ultimately burned Freud's books publicly and imprisoned and then executed four Jewish members of the Berlin Institute. By 1934, Hitler's dictatorship would bring the work of the Berlin Psychoanalytic Institute to an end.

Karen Horney's means of escape came in early 1932, when she received a telephone call from Franz Alexander, one of her former students. Alexander had moved to the United States and founded a center for psychoanalysis in Chicago. He wanted Karen Horney to come work alongside him. The decision was not hard to make. The German government was moving in a frightening direction. Her fellow Berlin psychoanalysts seemed uninterested in her female-centered ideas. Two of her daughters were out on their own, Marianne attending medical school and Brigitte moving into the limelight as an actress. Renate, 15, the youngest, could travel with her. In September 1932, mother and daughter boarded the ocean liner *Reliance*, crossed the Atlantic, and traveled to Chicago.

THE CHICAGO INSTITUTE FOR PSYCHOANALYSIS

As associate director of the Chicago Institute for Psychoanalysis, Karen Horney continued teaching and overseeing young analysts in training; she also saw patients of her own and continued research and writing. She came as an emissary of European psychoanalysis into a foreign land where Freud's ideas were not viewed as the be-all and end-all of psychological theory. Americans recognized Freud's importance in the field, but there was room for skepticism. The great American psychologist William James, who attended the five lectures Freud had delivered at Harvard in 1909, granted his importance but remarked that Freud gave him "the impression of a man obsessed with fixed ideas." [51]

For Karen Horney, the American atmosphere was perfect: she was honored for her close affiliation with Freud—she was, after all, just one remove from the great man, having gone through analysis with Karl Abraham, one of his students—yet she also found the freedom to express and develop her own ideas. She befriended people who, like her, would make history in the American social sciences: Karl Menninger, the distinguished Kansas psychiatrist who with his father and brother founded the world-renowned Menninger Clinic, and Margaret Mead, the anthropologist first recognized for her fieldwork on adolescent girls in primitive society. Also soon joining Horney's circle of friends was Erich Fromm, another German psychotherapist who had fled the coming Nazi regime.

Karen Horney charged into action in Chicago. She and Franz Alexander published a brochure within a month, describing the Institute for Psychoanalysis as "Dedicated to Increasing the Knowledge of the Psychic Processes of Man." Psychoanalysis deserved to be accepted as a genuine area of study in American universities, stated the brochure, since the "intelligent public" was finding it "as natural to consult a psychoanalyst concerning a psychosis or neurosis as it is to go to an ophthalmologist in the case of eye trouble." [52] A large part of Alexander and Horney's mission was to educate the larger public about the values of psychoanalysis, since the work could not proceed without people willing to pay for analysis. They established lecture series both for professionals who might come into contact with individuals needing therapy—social workers and teachers, for example—and for the general public. Karen Horney drew crowds with topics designed to interest women, such as her lecture on "The Mother's Conflicts as Expressed Toward the Child."

BROADENING THE FRAME

In her professional writing, Horney continued to focus on women's issues as well. In 1933 she published "The Overvaluation of Love," a lengthy discussion of the conflict between women's relations to men and to work. Since she was submitting the paper to the newly founded American *Psychoanalytic Quarterly*, she had to write in English, a language not her own. While this early 1933 article shows signs of her struggle with the vocabulary and syntax of the English language, Karen Horney's writing style soon became as graceful and direct in her new tongue as it had been in her old.

The premise of this important paper was that while modern society allowed women to find their own interests and pursue work on their own, traditional expectations still loomed large in both men's and women's minds. Deep down, women were still expected to be housewives and homebound mothers. Any woman who rejected, or even downplayed, her role as wife and mother was considered abnormal. The situation could cause severe conflicts within a woman's psyche. As Horney pointed out,

> women who nowadays obey the impulse to the independent development of their abilities are able to do so only at the cost of a struggle against both external opposition and such resistances within themselves as are created by an intensification of the traditional ideal of the exclusively sexual function of woman.
>
> It would not be going too far to assert that at the present time this conflict confronts every woman who ventures upon a career of her own and who is at the same time unwilling to pay for her daring with the renunciation of her femininity. The conflict in question is therefore one that is conditioned by the altered position of woman and confined to those women who enter upon or follow a vocation, who pursue special interests, or who aspired in general to an independent development of their personality. [53]

Women bound up with this conflict may obsessively seek a husband or form homosexual partnerships instead; they may see other women as rivals and consider themselves ugly and unlovable. They tend to overvalue their relationships with men, seeking their own self-assurance. They become ambitious, motivated by low self-esteem and rivalry with others, yet often sabotage their own success. "They think that they can be happy only through love," Horney sums up, "whereas, constituted as they are, they can never be, while on the other hand they have an ever-diminishing faith in the worth of their abilities." [54]

The paper reflected Horney's sensitivity to women's circumstances. To her fellow psychoanalysts, it also showed that she considered individual psychology to be the sum of both personal and social forces—not only, as the Freudians believed, the expression of inborn biological instincts shaped by

Women in Early Psychoanalysis

Several other women besides Karen Horney played important roles in the early years of psychoanalysis: Anna Freud, Helene Deutsch, and Melanie Klein.

Anna Freud was the youngest of Sigmund and Martha Freud's seven children, born in 1895. She was always closer to her father than to either her mother or her siblings. From early on, they attended professional meetings together. Educated as a teacher, she taught briefly, but illness kept her from steady work in schools. Most of her adult life was spent as her father's caretaker—physically, emotionally, and intellectually. Eventually she ran a school and guidance clinic for children and published one book, *The Ego and Mechanisms of Defense,* in 1936. In 1938 she founded the Hampstead Child Therapy Clinic in London.

Helene Deutsch, born in Poland in 1884, moved to Germany as a young woman and was soon inspired by Freud's book, *The Interpretation of Dreams.* With a medical degree from the University of Munich, she moved to Vienna to study and undergo psychoanalysis with Freud. Her book, *The Psychology*

early private childhood experiences. Culture greatly influences personality, Horney was beginning to understand. Her
new American setting allowed her to open her mind to this
new way of thinking, expanding the focus of the analyst from
the purely personal to the social as well.

Several years later, writing the introduction to her book,
New Ways in Psychoanalysis, she directly attributed these new
ideas to her move to Chicago.

> The greater freedom from dogmatic beliefs which I
> found in this country [the United States] alleviated the
> obligation of taking psychoanalytical theories for

of Women, published in two volumes in 1944 and 1945,
emphasizes the relationship with the mother as a girl's formative childhood experience. Society inhibits girls' activity and
aggression, making them turn inward. When a woman reaches
childbearing age, many deep patterns from her own infancy
ean reemerge, causing ambivalence toward pregnancy, child-
birth, and mothering—and starting the cycle all over again.

Melanie Klein was born in Vienna in 1882 and became a
member of the Berlin Psychoanalytic Institute in its early
days, along with Karen Horney. Klein specialized in working
with children and discovered that observing children as they
played comfortably with toys could reveal a great deal about
their psychological conditions. Two of Karen Horney's daughters, Marianne and Brigitte, underwent psychotherapy with
Klein. Like Horney, Klein received much criticism for her disagreements with Freud, particularly since her theories of child
psychology put her in direct intellectual conflict with Anna
Freud. She moved to London in 1927 and lived there until
her death in 1960.

granted, and gave me the courage to proceed along the lines which I considered right. Furthermore, acquaintance with a culture which in many ways is different from the European taught me to realize that many neurotic conflicts are ultimately determined by cultural conditions. [55]

Furthermore, she explained in the same passage, her new friends, representing the broader social sciences, were influencing her thought, especially social psychologist Erich Fromm, who in his writing directly criticized Freud for leaving out the impact of culture from his psychological theories.

FROM CHICAGO TO NEW YORK

Soon Karen Horney discovered that vicious arguments about theory could happen among American psychoanalysts just as easily as among Europeans. She found herself in the middle of an "American Analytical Civil War," as some were to call it, over the same issues—Freudian orthodox psychoanalysis versus new theories. Perhaps Karen Horney actually enjoyed conflict. Perhaps she was drawn to the more lively discussions and openness to new ideas that she sensed on the East Coast compared to Chicago. Or perhaps, as the wife of one of her colleagues hypothesized, "in no way could she ever remain second in command anywhere." [56] It was true, tensions had been building between Karen Horney and Franz Alexander.

For whatever reason, Karen Horney decided to leave Chicago after two years. She moved to New York, even though she had no job and no security: just connections and self-confidence. Once there, she applied for membership in the New York Psychoanalytic Institute, the most highly respected psychoanalytic organization in the United States, founded by A.A. Brill, who had translated Freud's writings into English. The application form asked for the names of her supervisors. She simply wrote, "As long as the institution of supervised analyses exists—since 1920—I have *done* supervising work." When asked for a list of the courses she had attended, she did the same: "As long as psychoanalytic training courses exist, I have *given* courses, such as lectures on technique, case-seminars, lectures on feminine psychology, etc." [57] In the long run, Karen Horney was admitted, but not, one imagines, without several pairs of raised eyebrows among those in power at the New York Institute.

Life in New York was soon a social whirl for Karen Horney. Karen and her daughter Renate moved into a fashionable new apartment building overlooking Central Park. She connected quickly with the city's circles of artists and intellectuals, many of whom were also German **émigrés**. Erich Fromm moved to New York at about the same time she did, and soon their friendship became a romantic relationship that was to last for years. She befriended Paul Tillich, a German philosopher and theologian, and his wife, Hannah, who had recently come to New York so he could teach at Union Theological Seminary. She and her friends spent many an evening together, eating and drinking, sometimes to excess, and debating psychology and philosophy into the wee hours of the night.

HORNEY'S NEW YORK CIRCLES

While Karen Horney's first professional connections were to the New York Psychoanalytic Institute, she soon established an affiliation with the New School for Social Research. An innovative **social science** research institute founded in 1918 by American intellectuals including John Dewey and Thorstein Veblen, by the 1930s the New School had added adult education to its mission. The school founded a program called "University in Exile" and became a magnet for Jewish social scientists and artists fleeing the Nazis. Located on East 12th Street in New York's Greenwich Village, the New School drew freethinkers, political radicals, daring artists, and original scholars. As Horney's biographer Susan Quinn wrote, "It is hard to imagine an institution better suited to Karen Horney's temperament than the New School." [58] She began to teach at the New School in 1935 and taught at least a course a year there for the rest of her life, offering public lectures and seminars with faculty from other disciplines as well.

In the mid-1930s, Karen Horney was nearing the age of 50. She stood only five feet, three inches tall and was rather thick-waisted. She had a round, jowly face and sad, heavy-lidded eyes. Her hair was becoming more silver than brown. At a glance, no one would find her physically attractive, and yet from all accounts, her personality charmed everyone, men and women. "She was not a beautiful woman," a friend recalled. "She was a little coy, she had a little of the actress in her. Her expression was so lively . . . her face was shining and she had wonderful hands, wonderful movements." Not just her friends but those who came to hear her lecture for the first time grew fascinated by Karen Horney's presence. "Everybody was just *hanging* on what she had to say," remembered her friend. "And standing applause. It was not just an *ordinary* talk, it was a very moving experience." [59]

Her magnetic personality helped draw patients to her for therapy, and within six months of her moving to New York, her practice was full. She was lecturing at the Psychoanalytic Institute, teaching at the New School, and commuting occasionally from New York to lecture on psychoanalytic technique for the Baltimore–Washington Society, considered a center for unorthodox thinking among psychoanalysts. Some of her best friends came from that renegade circle. A tightknit group of four began to meet more often, calling themselves the Zodiac Club: Karen Horney, Harry Stack Sullivan, now living in New York, Clara Thompson, and William Silverberg. (For more information on Clara Thompson, enter "Clara Thompson" into any search engine and browse the sites listed.) Thompson was an American, eight years younger than Horney, and the two women shared the experience of having fought their way into the male-dominated profession of psychiatry. Thompson had earned her M.D. at Johns Hopkins, then traveled to Europe several times for analysis with Sandor Ferenczi, a student of Freud's. Silverberg was an American who had spent two years of psychoanalytic training in Berlin.

The Zodiac four had great times together, talking heatedly over drinks and dinner, then going out on the town to jazz clubs or the theater. The more conservative members of the New York Psychiatric Society began to look askance at the group, suspicious of their tendency to bring ideas from **sociology**, **anthropology**, and **cultural studies** into psychoanalytic theory. Ironically, Karen Horney became an official member of the New York Psychoanalytic Society in 1935, at the same time that her social life, together with her ever more radical critiques of Freudian theory, were raising doubts about her in the minds of powerful members of that august organization.

Daring to Put
It in Writing

1935–1937

5

In 1935, Karen Horney offered a lecture series on "Culture and Neurosis." Its very title indicated the nontraditional direction in which her work was headed. Neurosis should be understood in the context of **culture**, she said, and not only, as strict Freudians would have it, the individual's childhood history. Horney was interested, as she stated in an article drawn from these lectures, in discovering "whether and to what extent neuroses are moulded by cultural processes in essentially the same way as 'normal' character formation is determined by these influences." [60]

Feelings of rivalry and competition lie at the heart of many psychological disturbances. To explain these feelings, a Freudian psychoanalyst would trace them back to early childhood longings for the mother or father, because Freud identified the very physical bonds between infant and parent as the first sexual attachments in every person's life. Horney did not deny these feelings, but she considered them less important than jealousies among adults that arose later in life. The neurotic individual, she suggested, is bound up with thoughts of self-comparison, always seeking to outdo others, striving for more than is possible, disappointed when fantasies of superiority do not come true, and hostile toward those who appear to be accomplishing more. This self-perpetuating cycle of dissatisfaction with self and envy toward others formed the core of a neurotic personality. A culture that rewards hard work, accomplishment, and winning over others fuels the fire and makes it likely that this particular neurosis will develop.

Two months later, Horney delivered her first public lecture at the New York Psychoanalytic Institute. Her title was "The Problem of the Negative Therapeutic Reaction." In this talk, prepared for an audience of psychoanalysts, Horney considered how the competitive neurotic reacts to the therapy situation, in which the analyst offers explanations for deviant behavior with the assumption that having learned all this, the patient ought to change. "These people are constantly wavering between rivalry and affection," she said of neurotic patients. To them, the therapy situation represents a competition. When the therapist comes up with a diagnosis, it's a winning move. The patient, refusing to let the therapist win, may refuse to hear it. Therapeutic solutions may feel like accusations or rejections, alienating the patient and actually slowing down the healing process. "Interpretations which connect the present difficulties immediately with influences in childhood are scientifically only half truths and practically useless," she dared to say. [61]

With this argument, Horney launched a careful attack on Freudian psychoanalysis. An exclusive focus on the childhood sources for neurosis is not the best solution, she was saying. Rivalry and affection may be childish inclinations. In adults, though, these feelings are "not direct repetitions or revivals of infantile attitudes, but have been changed in quality and quantity by the consequences which have developed out of the early experiences." [62] An adult patient cares more about what is happening in the present day and why, not about attachments that occurred in a time so early in life, he or she often cannot even remember them.

Horney knew that she needed to tread lightly in expressing these ideas to her orthodox audience. "It is needless to say— and I say it only because misunderstandings have arisen," she continued, "that this procedure does not mean that I attribute less importance to childhood experiences than any other analyst. These are of fundamental importance since they determine the direction of the individual's development." She saved the last word, though, for her own ideas: the essential role of adult experiences in neurotic personalities. She called them the "upper layers" of a personality and insisted that by working through them, the deeper memories could be reached. [63]

She delivered the same address in German to her former colleagues in Berlin when she went home for the holidays in

December 1935. No strong objections were voiced at either lecture. But when she proposed to the education committee of the New York Institute that she offer a course on changing techniques of psychoanalysis, her proposal was rejected. She responded with fury. "If there are reasons why my lectures are not considered desirable these should be stated frankly and I should accept them though I should be sorry as I feel, as do some of the students, that I have something constructive to offer," she wrote to the Institute's director. [64] She did have a faithful following of students—in fact, the strong attachments between Horney and her students worried some people at the Institute. Might she convince them, too, to depart from the strict Freudian path?

TIME TO WRITE A BOOK

Karen Horney knew that she had a message, and even if it rankled her colleagues at the New York Psychoanalytic Institute, others would benefit from hearing it. She began compiling her New School lectures on "Culture and Neurosis" into a book. She was still insecure about her English, but she kept her writing style simple and direct. "It is written in such a simple—though bad!—language," she wrote her editor, W.W. Norton, "that interested and educated laypersons can read it, and—I feel pretty sure—will read it, because it concerns their own problems." [65]

The Neurotic Personality of Our Time was published in 1937. In its short introduction, Karen Horney boldly proclaimed her departure from Freudian psychoanalysis. It stands as a clear description of the new approach that she introduced to the field of psychotherapy.

> Emphasis is put on the actually existing conflicts and the neurotic's attempts to solve them, on his actually existing anxieties and the defenses he has built up against them. This emphasis on the actual situation does not mean that

I discard the idea that essentially neuroses develop out of early childhood experiences. But I differ from many psychoanalytic writers inasmuch as I do not consider it justified to focus our attention on childhood in a sort of one-sided fascination and then consider later reactions essentially as repetitions of earlier ones. I want to show that the relation between childhood experiences and later conflicts is much more intricate than is assumed by those psychoanalysts who proclaim a simple cause and effect relationship. Though experiences in childhood provide determining conditions for neuroses they are nevertheless not the only cause of later difficulties. [66]

Neuroses, or behavioral abnormalities, do not just come out of a person's unique experience. They are also formed by the culture in which the person lives. "In fact," wrote Horney, "the cultural conditions not only lend weight and color to the individual experiences but in the last analysis determine their particular form." [67] She chose an example that had a long history in traditional Freudian analysis: the example of the man raised by a domineering or self-sacrificing woman. In the Freudian view, a boy raised by such a mother would develop deep-seated fears and angers toward her, feelings that would be repeated in his adult relationships with women, especially his wife. "But it is only under definite cultural conditions that we find domineering or self-sacrificing mothers," Horney wrote, "and it is only because of these existing conditions that such an experience will have an influence on later life." [68] Only in a culture that considers that women should be weaker and subordinate to men will a woman who acts otherwise seem to have a damaging effect on her son's personality. What appears unique in an individual's early history is really a part of the larger society or culture. It is something that everyone in that culture, not just the neurotic individual, experiences.

"When we realize the great import of cultural conditions on neuroses the biological and physiological conditions, which are considered by Freud to be their root, recede into the background," Horney argued. Only with "well-established evidence"—real memories recounted by the patient, not just theories about infantile instincts—should the therapist emphasize early problems over present-day ones. [67] "I believe that a strict adherence to all of Freud's theoretical interpretations entails the danger of tending to find in neuroses what Freud's theories lead one to expect to find," she dared to write. [70] As always, she took care to recognize how important Freud's work has been, but at the same time she insisted that those coming after him must explore new ideas: "I believe that deference for Freud's gigantic achievements should show itself in building on the foundations that he has laid, and that in this way we can help to fulfill the possibilities which psychoanalysis has for the future, as a theory as well as a therapy." [71]

One important new idea proposed by Horney in her first book was that childhood suffering or traumatic events may not, in fact, end up damaging a person and turning him or her neurotic. A traditional psychoanalyst assumed that every abnormal behavior could be traced back to some formative incident or relationship early in life, often so early that the patient didn't remember it. Forgotten moments of pain, separation, rejection, or jealousy toward one parent over the love of the other— personal and primitive events such as these festered inside the neurotic. The goal of analysis, the key step toward a cure, was to unveil and recognize those events or feelings.

Horney disagreed. "A child can stand a great deal of what is often regarded as traumatic," she wrote,

> as long as inwardly he feels wanted and loved. Needless to say, a child feels keenly whether love is genuine, and cannot be fooled by any faked demonstrations. The main reason why a child does not receive enough warmth

and affection lies in the parents' incapacity to give it on account of their own neuroses. More frequently than not, in my experience, the essential lack of warmth is camouflaged, and the parents claim to have in mind the child's best interests. [72]

Isolated traumatic events were not as formative as a general parental attitude of love, warmth, and acceptance. In the attachment between parent and child, strict Freudians tended to see primitive sexuality and considered it potentially destructive. Karen Horney instead saw nurturing warmth and self-affirming affection. In many ways, she was expressing the woman's— and the mother's—point of view.

KAREN HORNEY AS MOTHER

Karen Horney was 52 years old when her first book was published. All three of her daughters were adults, each a distinct personality. Brigitte, the oldest Horney daughter, still lived in Germany. Her acting career was soaring. She starred in a patriotic German film, translated for American audiences as *A Man Wants to Get to Germany,* dramatizing the efforts of a brave World War I soldier to get from South Africa back home to Germany. Her tall, slender body and dark, sultry eyes meant that she was often typecast as the romantic heroine, sometimes set in the present day but also sometimes set back more than a century, in the dashing Napoleonic era. She performed in 27 films altogether between 1930 and 1943, becoming a household name among Germans and continuing on to stage and television. (For more information on "Brigitte Horney," enter her name into any search engine and browse the sites listed.)

Marianne, the second daughter, had moved to the United States, and she and her sister Renate had stayed in Chicago when Karen moved to New York. Marianne followed in her mother's professional footsteps. She completed her courses for a medical degree in Germany, then enrolled at the University of

Chicago for further clinical training in psychiatry. She received her M.D. in 1935, interned in Chicago, then became a psychiatric resident in a clinic in New York. She had not planned it that way but now, living in New York, Marianne Horney was able to attend some of her mother's lectures at the New School. Surely feelings of pride and competition mingled inside her. In 1936, Karen Horney suggested that her daughter undergo psychoanalysis as a valuable step in training to be a therapist. She urged Marianne to choose Erich Fromm as her analyst. Years later, Marianne said that her work with Fromm had "unblocked" parts of her personality and helped her find "the capacity for growth." [73] During her two years of therapy, though, she lashed out at her mother, expressing anger she had never revealed before. Karen Horney blamed Erich Fromm, believing that he had used Marianne to express his own angry feelings toward his friend and lover. It was a complicated relationship that most psychotherapists would not have allowed to happen.

Renate, the youngest, chose the more traditional female path, moving back to Germany after several years in Chicago and marrying her childhood sweetheart. Renate had a daughter in 1936, and she named her Kaya, Karen Horney's childhood nickname. The new grandmother visited Germany as often as possible. In 1937, she brought something special for Renate and Kaya. Karen Horney could see how life was becoming more difficult in Germany. The Nazi regime was closing in, the economy was struggling, and the German people were making do with very little. Dairy products were nearly impossible to find. Karen Horney kept her Christmas surprise a secret for days, hiding it outside in the snow. On Christmas morning, she brought the gift inside and placed it under the tree: ten pints of whipping cream and seven pounds of butter! "Never in my life did I taste whipped cream as good as that," Renate recalled years later. [74]

But Karen Horney worried about Renate. Her husband, Fredy Crevenna, dreamed of becoming a film director, but that

Erich Fromm

Erich Fromm was born in Frankfurt, Germany, within months of the publication of Sigmund Freud's first landmark book, *The Interpretation of Dreams.* He grew up a generation after Freud, and was one of the first, along with Karen Horney, to feel driven to carry Freud's pioneering ideas a step further and to see them in the larger light of society and history. He was particularly influenced by the ideas and writing of Karl Marx, who saw human history in terms of economics and power. Fromm received a Ph.D. in sociology—not a medical degree—from the University of Heidelberg, which made him suspect as a psychoanalyst among strict Freudians, even though he underwent training at the Berlin Psychoanalytic Institute. Along with so many other German intellectuals, he moved to the United States in 1934.

Fromm once described his approach as a "dynamic analysis of the economic, political, and psychological forces that form the basis of society." * His first and perhaps most famous book, *Escape from Freedom,* published in 1941, wrote abstractly about the human tendency to "escape from" responsibility and rewards, not "escape to" higher goals. "Freedom from the traditional bonds of medieval society, though giving the individual a new feeling of independence, at the same time made him feel alone and isolated, filled him with doubt and anxiety, and drove him into new submission and into a compulsive and irrational activity," Fromm wrote.** He considered this a distinctly modern trait, and many saw his book as a commentary on the German people. The doubt and anxiety that came from their modern freedom led them to support the authoritarian government delivered by Hitler and the Nazis.

Fromm taught at many universities in the United States and Mexico and published more than 30 books, including one each on Freud and Marx. He died in 1980.

* Rainer Funk, "Erich Fromm's Life and Work," website of the International Erich Fromm Society [http://www.erichfromm.de/english/life/life_bio2.html].

** Erich Fromm, *Escape from Freedom* (New York: Farrar & Rinehart, 1941), 89.

ambition was going nowhere. He was proving to be a domineering husband, leaving Renate afraid to argue, disagree, or make decisions without his approval. Karen sensed the situation. She talked privately with both Renate and Fredy, but there was little more she could do to make their marriage better. She did encourage them to move out of Germany, but escape from their Nazi homeland became more and more difficult through the 1930s. The United States set quotas on immigrants, so moving to New York was out of the question. They moved to Mexico, and soon Karen Horney had a second grandchild.

REACTIONS TO HER BOOK

Most readers and reviewers responded positively to *The Neurotic Personality of Our Time*. Franz Alexander, Horney's past colleague in Chicago, reviewed the book for the *Psychoanalytic Quarterly* and congratulated the author for her "independent, scrutinizing attitude, uninfluenced by accepted abstractions." He wrote that she was helping the whole psychiatric profession by "counteracting a current trend to substitute theoretical abstractions for psychological understanding." [75] John Dollard, a sociologist, reviewed the book for a scholarly journal as well, writing that "Dr. Horney is at her best in the stubborn thinking-through and literal realistic expression of the actual present-day character structure of her patients" [76]— exactly what she intended her book to emphasize. The anthropologist Margaret Mead wrote a letter to Horney, congratulating her friend on her "creative hypothesis" and comparing it to "a road that leads out from a confined little walled town on to an open plain." [77] Clara Thompson, praising Horney's new approach, still predicted that the book would "arouse controversy in analytical circles." [78]

Orthodox Freudians criticized the book, as might be expected. Ernest Jones, who would become Sigmund Freud's biographer, complained that in Horney's theory, infantile sexuality "recedes into the background." Another Freudian wrote that Horney seemed to "treat disdainfully the established facts of infantile psycho-sexual drives," thereby giving "the false impression that her excellent analysis of ego defenses and attitudes is all of psychoanalysis that is important." Another turned Freudian lines of thought back on Horney, suggesting that her critique was a veiled expression of anger against male authority. "Since so much of Dr. Horney's work is concerned with hostility," he wrote, "it is interesting to note the ill-concealed hostility toward Freud and other analysts through this section of the work." [79] Faithful followers were feeling particularly protective toward Sigmund Freud in 1937, considering that the grand old man of psychoanalysis was fighting cancer, still living in Vienna, a potential target for the Nazis in Austria. A year later, at the age of 82, Freud moved to London to live out the last year of his life.

Out and
On Her Own

1938–1940

6

THE CHANGING PERSONALITY OF PSYCHOANALYSIS

In October 1938, German troops invaded Austria in March and Czechoslovakia in October. The year marked a turning point in the world's understanding of the meaning of Adolf Hitler and his Nazi regime. Hitler demanded that a portion of Czechoslovakia be allowed to join Germany. Britain and France, wanting to avoid international conflict, backed his demand. But once he had that portion of Czechoslovakia, Hitler demanded more. Clearly his intention was to extend his country's boundaries and to force more of Europe to follow his anti-Semitic laws, which since 1933 had been growing more stringent and inhumane, depriving Jews of their citizenship, restricting their freedoms, and allowing the government to seize their wealth and property. Jewish liberties were shattered on the night called *Kristallnacht*, November 9–10, 1938. Rioters in Germany, Austria, Poland, and Czechoslovakia, incited by Nazi leaders, burned Jewish synagogues, vandalized Jewish schools and cemeteries, and destroyed Jewish-owned businesses. On that night, tens of thousands were arrested just because they were Jewish and sent to concentration camps.

All told, 1938 was a year of horrors, especially for Jews still living in Germany, Austria, Czechoslovakia, and Poland. By the end of that year, it is estimated that more than half of all the Jewish people in Germany had fled their homeland. Tens of thousands moved to the United States. Numerous organizations formed to help them. The New York Psychoanalytic Society established its own Emergency Committee on Relief and Immigration. Karen Horney, when asked to join, declined. To others, she appeared not to care, and they criticized her for it. The fact is, she was spending time, effort, and money helping to relocate those she knew personally, as she had helped Renate and her family.

Many of the Jewish refugees were intellectuals, including doctors and psychiatrists. Their presence made a difference in professional circles in America. On the one hand, organizations like the New York Psychoanalytic Society and Institute felt the need to tighten their entrance requirements, to be sure that new members did indeed fit in. Those who were accepted as members tended to be conservative, representing the old school of European psychoanalysis. The atmosphere at the New York Psychoanalytic Society shifted, creating a situation where Karen Horney's new ideas were not as easily accepted as they might have been even five years before, when she first arrived.

REJECTED

In many ways, Karen Horney was at the peak of her career in the late 1930s. She taught at several schools. She offered popular lectures. She supervised student analysts in training and developed strong relationships with them. Her ideas were strong and significant. They sparked debate, attracted many followers, and provoked some critics. She had become an influential, if controversial, voice in the field of psychology. She had written one successful book and was now publishing a second, *New Ways in Psychoanalysis.* She had good friends and enjoyed socializing in her apartment on Central Park West. Friends from these days recalled the little roulette wheel she kept in her living room. Evenings at Karen's often turned into lighthearted gambling parties with pennies for stakes. Erich Fromm would sometimes sing for the group, chiming out the Hebrew songs he had learned as a child in Germany.

It was during these days of accomplishment and satisfaction that Karen Horney gave her talk to the members of the New York Psychoanalytic Society on "The Emphasis of Genesis in Freud's Thinking." One month later, the membership reconvened for further discussion of her presentation, and the conversation devolved into insults and accusations. Horney sat there dumbfounded, hearing her colleagues publicly lambast her and her ideas. That episode in November 1939, the one time her friends ever saw Karen Horney shed tears, was just the beginning of her troubles with the New York Psychoanalytic Society.

New rules were formulated by the Society's education committee early in 1940. "All basic changes in viewpoint on matters of theory" had to be cleared by the membership before being offered to students." [80] The committee would decide at what point in a student's education such new and divergent ideas would be introduced. It had been the practice that students could select their own training analysts from the faculty. Now, the education committee ruled, trainers would be assigned to students. All these rules were designed to minimize the influence of innovative ideas on the students.

Then some of Karen Horney's students found that other faculty members at the New York Psychoanalytic Institute were finding fault with the papers they were writing, even those that Horney had edited and approved. At the Institute, as in any other graduate school, an important final step in student's education was to research and write an original thesis, showing his or her work and ideas in the field. Fourteen of Horney's students, having made it successfully to this stage, received negative comments on their theses. Graders wrote that they were rejecting the papers for "not being analytic enough" [81]—code language that the students clearly understood as "not being Freudian enough"—and that only with revisions would they be allowed to pass. Three of the students, outraged, actually chose not to rewrite their theses along more Freudian lines.

One other event seemed to single out Karen Horney for criticism. A faculty member originally from Vienna, Fritz Wittels, sent a long, angry letter to every member of the Psychoanalytic Society, stating that in her new book, Horney "with one sweeping gesture . . . refuted most of the fundamentals of psychoanalysis." Its enthusiastic reception by the general public showed how eager the average person is to deny that "our sex life is of fundamental importance in the structure of human psychology," wrote Wittels, and the result was that "forty years of patient scientific work was thrown to the dogs." Wittels went on to state that "all experienced analysts" found *New Ways in Psychoanalysis* "absurd in its essentials." He accused her of trying to "smash Freud's psychoanalysis in his own stronghold" and of surrounding herself "with a group of younger and youngest members of our psychoanalytic society" who know little about Freud but are threatening to take over the organization. In conclusion, Wittels demanded that either Horney return to the Freudian fold or go somewhere else to teach her version of, as he called it, "Social Psychotherapy." [82]

The letter set many Society members on edge. At their next meeting, they willingly agreed to the education committee's rules to exert more control over the content being taught their students. At that meeting, Karen Horney requested that the membership discuss Wittels's letter as a group, but no one followed her suggestion. Soon her routine request to teach a course on new techniques was rejected. Students spoke up, telling the education committee that they felt intimidated by the faculty, who forced them to follow the orthodox Freudian view. The students' concerns were not taken seriously, however, and they responded by presenting a set of resolutions that argued against the decisions being made by those in charge.

The administration of the New York Psychoanalytic Institute seemed driven to uphold a "serious scientific fallacy," wrote the students, namely

that what is historically early in the development of psychoanalysis is automatically fundamental, and must therefore be thoroughly inculcated in the student before permitting him to become acquainted with later development and trends. This is equivalent to insisting that a student in chemistry or physics be thoroughly indoctrinated with the early theories of the constitution of matter before permitting him any contact with the atomic theory. [83]

In short, argued the students, the education committee had taken "the profoundly unscientific position that nothing new has been or can be developed in psychoanalytic theory and practice beyond the original teachings of Freud." [84]

THE STUDENTS SPEAK OUT

Frustrated by the factionalism he saw among his colleagues, child psychiatrist David Levy took matters into his own hands. Throughout the conflicts between Karen Horney and the powerful leaders of the New York Psychoanalytic Society, David Levy worked very hard to remain a balanced mediator, respecting both sides. At the time, he was president of the American Psychoanalytic Association, a national organization, and he genuinely wanted to heal the wounds within his profession. Ultimately, he supported Karen Horney and her friends in their arguments that they had been unfairly treated—an indication that, although she may have had a difficult personality, Horney did not deserve the treatment she received.

After the education committee dismissed the student resolutions, David Levy found a scientific way to canvass all the students of the Institute, testing the committee's theory that their complaints were not valid. In February 1941, he distributed a survey to all students of the Institute, asking four questions. Had they ever been intimidated by an instructor or society member? Had they ever been advised to avoid a particular course because it would harm their chances of gaining membership to the society? Had they ever been advised to avoid a particular training analyst for the same reason? And, finally, even if they had not received such warnings, had their choice of training analyst been made with such concerns in mind? Students could complete the survey anonymously, and they were invited to write any further comments if they wished.

Of the 110 students currently in training at the New York Psychoanalytic Institute, 72 responded. About one-third of them answered "yes" to one or more of the questions, indicating that they had felt some sort of intimidation from faculty members. A few complained that they were annoyed by the non-traditional student clique. "They frequently egg each other on to deliver opposing points of view to the assembled group," one person wrote, "and these points of view are always anti-Freudian." [85] More, though, complained of influences coming at them from the other direction.

Several felt that their papers had been criticized for unorthodox content, not for quality of work and ideas. The atmosphere even influenced their choice of research topics, wrote one. He had attended Society meetings where he "witnessed scenes in which some of those who disagreed with [Dr. Horney's] views have displayed such animus that no calm and decent consideration of the scientific issues was given." After such meetings, students talking among themselves agreed that to succeed on their assignments, they had "only to show a rote intellectualized grasp of the principles of classical Freudian psychoanalysis but not any critical thought departing from tradition." [86] Another student reported that the education committee reversed their positive judgment of his work just days after he participated in writing the student resolutions. "I cannot understand how any group of men who are supposed to be psychoanalyzed themselves can establish themselves as a hierarchical body with the aim of directing the thought processes of adult students along a prescribed groove," wrote a student on his questionnaire.[87] Summing up the student responses, David Levy called it "an appalling situation." [88]

Lawrence Kubie, the director of the Society and Institute, minimized Levy's concerns. He blamed the students' discontent on Karen Horney. Their problems, he reported in writing, were "due entirely to the fact that the minds of certain students are being poisoned by hostile and irresponsible members of the Society." [89] The war was escalating, and Kubie had the upper hand. In April 1941, he announced the education committee's decision to demote Karen Horney. She would no longer be an instructor at the New York Psychoanalytic Institute. She would be given the lower-ranking title of lecturer, which implied that her teaching assignments—and her power at the school—would shrink considerably. The statement was read aloud before the members. One faculty member dared to stand up and publicly question "the wisdom of the course." [90] Still, when the full membership voted, the decision to demote Karen Horney passed, 24 to 7. Many members abstained from voting altogether.

Karen Horney stood up and walked out of the meeting room. Four others followed her, including her friend Clara Thompson. Two days later, the same five addressed a single short letter to the secretary of the Society:

> For the last few years, it has become gradually more apparent that the scientific integrity of the New York Psychoanalytic Society has steadily deteriorated. Reverence for dogma has replaced free inquiry; academic freedom has been abrogated; students have been intimidated; scientific sessions have degenerated into political machinations.
>
> When an instructor and training analyst is disqualified solely because of scientific convictions, any hopes we may have harbored for improvement in the policies of the society have been dispelled.
>
> We are interested only in the scientific advancement of psychoanalysis in keeping with the courageous spirit

of its founder, Sigmund Freud. This obviously cannot be achieved within the framework of the New York Psycho-analytic Society as it is now constituted.

Under the circumstances, we have no alternative but to resign, however much we may regret the necessity for this action. [91]

The Phoenix of
Psychoanalysis

1940–1944

7

FOUNDING AN ALTERNATIVE

In less than a month, Karen Horney, Clara Thompson, and their allies founded a new professional society. They named it the Association for the Advancement of Psychoanalysis (AAP) and celebrated their victory at Karen Horney's house. They toasted one another and sang the popular song of the day from George Gershwin's opera *Porgy and Bess,* "It Ain't Necessarily So." Soon they published a journal, the *American Journal of Psychoanalysis,* which listed 15 charter AAP members and promised courses to be taught the following year through AAP and the New School. By the fall, AAP had instituted training courses in psychoanalysis. "Students are acknowledged to be intelligent and responsible adults," the AAP literature stated. The new society intended "to avoid conceptual rigidities, and to respond to ideas, whatever the source, in a spirit of scientific and academic democracy." [92] The energetic new group attracted luminaries into its fold, including Horney's close friends Erich Fromm and Harry Stack Sullivan. (For more information on "Harry Stack Sullivan," enter his name into any search engine and browse the sites listed.)

Exhilarating opportunities opened up to Karen Horney through her new association. Now she could partner with others and apply the ideas of social science to the real-life issues of the day—and there were plenty of issues for Americans to worry about in those days. The formation of AAP coincided almost exactly with the Japanese bombing of Pearl Harbor. The war in Europe may have been nearing a close, but war in the Pacific was raging. Horney wrote a paper on the "Understanding of Individual Panic" that showed that while panic reactions to emergencies may have links to childhood anxieties, the treatment of them needs to happen at a social, not an individual, level, focusing on present-day fears rather than childhood memories. Newspapers like the *New York Post* picked up on the lecture and broadcast its practical advice to millions. Within the month, Karen Horney's third book appeared in bookstores.

She began this book, titled *Self-Analysis*, by tracing the evolution of psychoanalysis from its medical beginnings to its broader social implications, which she championed. For Freud, psychoanalysis was a method of therapy treating those physical disorders that seemed to have no physical cause—phobias, depression, drug addiction, for example. Analysts after him began to understand that "many people have personality disorders without showing any of the definite symptoms that had previously been regarded as characteristic of neuroses." [93] Even more broadly, psychoanalysis came to be recognized as something that could help even those who did not suffer from psychological disorders. "To an increasing degree people turn to analysis not because they suffer from depressions, phobias, or comparable disorders but because they feel they cannot cope with life or feel that factors within themselves are holding them back or injuring their relationships with others," wrote Horney. In short, many had come to believe that psychoanalysis could aid in "general character development." [94]

Horney didn't mean this to be a popular self-improvement book, like Dale Carnegie's *How to Win Friends and Influence People,* the famous advice book written in 1936. She was suggesting self-analysis for people already involved in psychoanalysis with a professional, as a way to extend the process or keep working between meetings. Reviewers didn't understand it that way, though. A writer for the *New Republic* called her book "the key to self-analysis for three dollars." [95] Once again, Karen Horney's ideas were misunderstood. But now, with a circle of believers around her, she protected herself from the pain of rejection.

TWO THEMES OF *SELF-ANALYSIS*

In her book's discussion of the need for self-analysis, Horney listed ten "neurotic trends" that warranted attention. After summarizing definitions of neurosis offered by Freud, Adler, and Jung, she presented her own. "In the center of psychic disturbances," she believed, "are unconscious strivings developed in order to cope with life despite fears, helplessness, and isolation." She granted that this definition is no more solid and absolute than any other. "Every explorer into the unknown has some vision of what he expects to find . . . Discoveries have been made even though the vision was incorrect. This fact may serve as consolation for the uncertainty of our present psychological knowledge." [96] Neurotic trends are unconscious forces, little recognized by the person driven by them, and they lead to imbalanced and **compulsive behaviors**. By tracing those behaviors back to the neurotic trends, self-analysis can lead to improved psychological health.

Horney listed these ten trends:

1. The neurotic need for affection and approval;

2. The neurotic need for a "partner who will take over one's life";

3. The neurotic need to restrict one's life within narrow borders;

4. The neurotic need for power: to control self and others through reason and foresight, or to believe in the omnipotence of will;

5. The neurotic need to exploit others and by hook or crook get the better of them;

6. The neurotic need for social recognition or prestige;

7. The neurotic need for personal admiration;

8. The neurotic ambition for personal achievement;

9. The neurotic need for self-sufficiency and independence; and

10. The neurotic need for perfection and unassailability.

As Horney pointed out, every one of these needs is a normal human desire. A need becomes neurotic when it is hollow, one-sided, and compulsive. The individual with a neurotic need for affection neither feels nor gives it, for example; the individual with a neurotic need for perfection is frightened of change, so will not put effort into getting better.

Throughout her book, Horney discusses the case of a woman named Clare, identified early on as "an actual patient" of hers. What those who knew her recognized—and what she admitted some years later—was that Clare was basically Horney herself, with a few features changed or added to make her a useful example for the book. Clare's childhood certainly, except for a few details, seemed to mirror that of Karen Danielsen. Her insights into Clare's personality represented Karen Horney's own self-analysis.

> She was an unwanted child. The marriage was unhappy. After having one child, a boy, the mother did not want any more children. Clare was born after several unsuccessful attempts at an abortion. She was not badly treated or neglected in any coarse sense: she was sent to schools as good as those the brother attended, she received as many gifts as he did, she had music lessons with the same teacher, and in all material ways was treated as well. But in less tangible matters she received less than the brother, less tenderness, less interest in school marks and in the thousand little daily experiences of a child, less concern when she was ill, less solicitude to have her around, less willingness to treat her as a confidante, less admiration for her looks and accom-plishments. . . . The father was no help. He was absent most of the time, being a country doctor. Clare made some pathetic attempts to get close to him but he was not interested in either of the children. . . . he was no help because he was openly despised by the mother, who

was sophisticated and attractive and beyond doubt the dominating spirit in the family. The undisguised hatred and contempt the mother felt for the father, including open death wishes against him, contributed much to Clare's feeling that it was much safer to be on the powerful side. [97]

Written by a woman nearly 60 years old about her own childhood, the passage seemed an explanation for much of the drive that had propelled Karen Horney through her troubled yet triumphant career.

THE RISE OF AAP

For its first year, 1941–1942, the Association for the Advancement of Psychoanalysis operated just as a professional society ought to. It organized a series of speakers, featuring a number of eminent scholars, most of whom had already figured into the life story of Karen Horney: anthropologist Margaret Mead; Chicago psychiatrist Franz Alexander; Adam Kardiner and David Levy, both still members of the New York Psychoanalytic Society. An ambitious convention took place in Boston in the spring of 1942, called "annual" even though it was the first ever. An affiliated school, the American Institute for Psychoanalysis, was founded to offer the AAP version of analysis training. It attracted new students, including Karen Horney's daughter, now married and teaching at Cornell Medical School in New York City. Three courses were offered, taught by Karen Horney, Clara Thompson, and William Silverberg. Other classes connected with AAP were offered at the New School. A healthy number of students enrolled.

"What Freud founded has already become greater than Freud," stated Silverberg, the association's first president, in the fall of 1941. "Psychoanalysis is not merely a therapeutic method; it is a psychology, and as such infiltrates into and illuminates every field in which an understanding of human nature is important." [98] AAP members became identified as psychologists and psychiatrists interested in the intersection of psychoanalysis with other social sciences. Its members researched topics such as the underlying psychological reasons for a person to become unemployed.

In many ways, the speedy organization of AAP was a miracle, and it showed the energy of Karen Horney and the others who were willing to break away from tradition and find new paths for psychoanalysis. In other ways, though, their swift success caused problems. Providing classes and training right away meant that they had to call on the more advanced students to teach the younger. The association had no building of its own, so they got permission to use rooms in the New York Medical College's teaching hospital. Horney and her friends pressed on through all of these inconveniences. The problems they could not surmount, though, were those that came at them from the New York Psychoanalytic Society and Institute.

ATTACKED BY THE ESTABLISHMENT

Monitoring the success of AAP, Lawrence Kubie, director of the New York Psychoanalytic, decided in the fall of 1941 that he needed to set the record straight. He crafted a statement on behalf of the Society, published it in the *Psychoanalytic Review,* and mailed copies to everyone who might take an interest. He even mailed it to allies of Karen Horney such as her editor W. W. Norton and her friend Margaret Mead.

He wrote that he wished to clear the air of the "unfounded allegations" made by those who had resigned from his organization in the spring. There were no grounds for accusations about prejudice against unorthodox theories, no reasons to claim student intimidation, he wrote. Instead, the controversy arose when new psychoanalytic theories were presented to young students, causing confusion, supporting an "unscientific tendency to form cliques," and encouraging them to "make radical technical departures" from the Institute's primary program. Finally, Kubie stated, Karen Horney had not been deprived of her academic freedom. She had not been expelled. The education committee had only "shifted the impact of her teaching from elementary . . . to intermediate and advanced" students. It was the dissident group—Horney and her friends—who "violated academic freedom by attempting to maintain an exclusive influence on the education of a small group of students." [99]

Kubie went further. He arranged to talk to a number of local psychoanalytic groups, further explaining the points in his written statement. Most groups welcomed him. The Baltimore–Washington Society said he could come only if he allowed Clara Thompson to speak at the same meeting, and he declined.

The AAP faced a political problem. Only if the national organization, the American Psychoanalytic Association, recognized its training program as legitimate, though, would it be able to grow and attract more students. The big test came with the election of APA's next president in the spring of 1942. The two candidates were William Silverberg, Karen Horney's ally, and Karl Menninger, an old acquaintance of Horney but a relatively conservative psychoanalyst. Menninger won the election. His acceptance speech, although tempered, showed where he stood on the issue of Horney and the AAP. "For the sake of dignity, unity, and prestige, scientific differences of opinion must be confined to the halls of our meeting places," he said. He criticized anyone who would carry professional disagreements into the general public "to obtain popular support by appealing to the prejudices and so-called common sense of persons unfamiliar with the details and history of science." [100] He meant Karen Horney. In short, the American Psychoanalytic Association under Menninger would not support an alternative professional society.

The decree voiced by Menninger and backed by the APA membership left a black mark on Karen Horney and her organization. Without acceptance at the national level, their training did not qualify students for official positions as analysts, their research would not be accepted by major journals, and their members would not be invited to meetings and conventions. It was, as one of Horney's biographers put it, a "brutal and complete exclusion from the parent organization of psychoanalysis." [101]

AAP BEGINS TO SCATTER

Crises erupted from within the Association as well. In a move that surprised everyone, Karen Horney ejected Erich Fromm from membership. Her stated reason was that he was not a physician and therefore should not be allowed to train future analysts. She told people that she wanted to keep AAP's standards high, so that the organization could soon partner with a medical school. Letting a non-M.D. teach might give reason for outsiders to doubt the quality of education offered.

Students went up in arms on behalf of Erich Fromm, just as they had three years earlier on behalf of Karen Horney. When the decision held and Fromm was no longer allowed to teach, a number of important people left the organization—including Marianne Horney Eckardt and Clara Thompson. Those who knew Karen Horney well suspected that complicated personal reasons drove her decision. She and Fromm had recently ended their years-long intimate relationship. Marianne had just completed four years of analysis with Fromm as well, and as a result of the analysis she had become more vocally critical of her mother. While Karen Horney offered official reasons for ejecting Erich Fromm, she probaby had personal motivations to criticize and perhaps even hurt him.

Another argument divided forces just a few months later. AAP officers had been discussing a connection with the New York Medical College. Karen Horney worried that the merger would mean AAP officials would lose too much control over their courses. Bitter disagreements surfaced, then the New York Medical College gave up on the plan. Again more members quit AAP, this time including William Silverberg. That meant that by early 1944, the three original founders of AAP had gone in separate directions. The Association for the Advancement of Psychiatry and its American Institute for Psychoanalysis survived, primarily through the steel will of Karen Horney and the dedication of a few of her followers. Horney taught, offered classes and lectures, and continued seeing patients in analysis. In some ways, the next few years went more smoothly because circumstances allowed her to be totally in charge.

8 Her Last Words

1944–1952

KAREN HORNEY'S PRIVATE LIFE

When she wrote Karen Horney's biography, author Susan Quinn interviewed a number of people who knew and worked with her directly. Patients from the mid-1940s offered colorful details about what it was like to arrive at Dr. Horney's apartment for a psychoanalysis appointment. By this time in her life, she saw patients only three times a week. Her first patient arrived at 5:30 in the morning. Patients entered into the the dining room, which doubled as the waiting room. All the windows were wide open, even in winter, so the apartment was frigid. Copies of *Gourmet* magazine were set out for patients to read. The dining table was covered with manuscripts, evidence of Horney's increasing dedication to her books. When Dr. Horney would appear, so would Butschi, her cocker spaniel, bounding out of her office door and wagging his tail. Sometimes he lay at Horney's feet during an appointment. Sometimes, mid-appointment, the housekeeper would knock on the door and take him out for a walk. Inside her office, books were stacked high everywhere.

She had always lived a life of the mind, but she had never denied the life of the body, either. There had been many men in Karen Horney's life, including many love affairs. Now in her sixties, she still had a boyfriend, a man considerably younger than she was. She spent more and more time with women friends as she grew older, though. One who became a constant companion was Gertrude Lederer-Eckardt, mother-in-law to her daughter Marianne. Gertrude, also German by birth, had twice been married. Her second husband had died soon before she met Marianne. Trained in physical education, Gertrude led exercise classes at the Cornell Medical Center, where Marianne worked and met her. Before long, new relationships were developing. Marianne fell in love and married Gertrude's son. Karen and Gertrude became fast friends. Over the years, they did more and more together—first socialized, then kept house, then bought a new house.

They found a little vacation cottage with a small garden in a subdivision called Wildwood Hills on southern Long Island, New York. Soon Karen and Gertrude, and any friends who would come with them, spent every weekend there. It became a routine. "Ten minutes before one o'clock," wrote Gertrude Lederer-Eckardt, "I stood waiting for [Karen] with the car before 240 Central Park South. Then, Sofie [Karen's house-keeper] came down with a basket of food on one arm, and the reluctant Butschi being dragged on his leash, laundry, books, and what not balanced on the other arm. And right after her Karen appeared, already in slacks, mostly still munching on her luncheon sandwich, so not to miss one single minute of her precious free weekend." [102]

Many believed that—except for her writing—playtime meant more than worktime during these last years of Karen Horney's life. Her daughter Renate lived with her husband and three children in Mexico. Karen often would stay with them for months at a time in the summer. She would prepare her daughter for the visit by saying she had been working too hard and needed to come to Mexico to do nothing. But Renate knew that Karen Horney's "nothing" was anybody else's busy schedule. "I knew it meant that she would keep me busy shopping, picnicking, touring, playing cards, you name it, . . . something all the time," said Renate. "Everything had to be structured, she could not completely relax, ever." [103]

HER LAST BOOKS

Karen Horney produced three more books in the years between 1945 and 1950. *Our Inner Conflicts,* published in 1945, continued to develop the theme that neurosis arose when an individual struggled with contradictory feelings or urges. They began as "contradictory attitudes toward others" but developed problematically into "contradictory attitudes toward the self, contradictory qualities and contradictory sets of values." [104] Horney outlined four ways that neurotics handle their inner conflicts: (1) by eclipsing them, which emphasizes a person's dependency on others; (2) by distancing oneself from others; (3) by distancing from oneself; and (4) by shifting responsibility for problems onto others. The goal of psychotherapy is to help the patient come to terms with his or her predominant coping strategy, then reduce that behavior so the person can more clearly know and express the "real self." This has happened once a person finds the "capacity to learn from his experiences—that is, if he can examine his share in the difficulties that arise, understand it, and apply the insight to his life." [105] In a sense, Horney was saying that successful psychoanalysis results in a life guided by self-analysis.

Working with other psychoanalysts, Horney next produced a book titled *Are You Considering Psychoanalysis?*, another effort to explain the value of psychological self-exploration to the general public. She and five AAP members wrote chapters on deciding to undergo analysis, choosing an analyst, and making the most of your decision. Horney's chapters were titled "What Does the Analyst Do?" and "How Do You Progress After Analysis?" The second reiterated the concepts of self-analysis that had become so important in her work.

Her editor at the publishing company now named for W.W. Norton, who had died in 1945, wanted Horney to write another book on her own. "I'm rather hoping you are again getting the itch to bring another book into being," he wrote. "We'd love to see another solo flight from you." [106] From her publisher's point of view, Karen Horney's writing style suited the educated, non-expert reading public. She had a knack for writing short, direct, easily understood explanations of relatively complex psychological ideas. She tended to write short books, which the public preferred. She used examples that were lifelike, inviting easy identification with the people she described. She avoided technical terminology and emphasized the application of psychological theory to the ordinary person's life. In a sense, Karen Horney's books form a bridge between the sophisticated, technical writings of psychiatric experts and the simpleminded advice books based on common sense and not much more. She could carry sound medical and psychological information into the arena of everyday life. Her books sold well and, she and her publishers believed, made a difference in the lives of the people who read them.

Her final book, published in 1950, titled *Neurosis and Human Growth,* was in many ways a summation of all that she had written before. It did take a step forward, though, in that Horney allowed herself to go beyond the descriptive and state that psychoanalysis and self-analysis were not simply a good idea but necessary processes for becoming a full human being. "To work at ourselves becomes not only the prime moral obligation," she wrote in the introduction, "but at the same time, in a very real sense, the prime moral *privilege.*" [107] Despite the moralistic tone, Horney's last book received praise from reviewers. Ashley Montagu, the physical anthropologist, writing in the *New York Herald Tribune,* called it "the author's most important book since *The Neurotic Personality of Our Time.*" [108]

TO JAPAN FOR HER LAST ADVENTURE

A new strand of thought emerged in Horney's later books: her increasing interest in the wisdom of Zen Buddhism. "In Zen Buddhist writings," she wrote in *Our Inner Conflicts,* "sincerity is equated with wholeheartedness, pointing to the very conclusion we reach on the basis of clinical observation—namely, that nobody divided within himself can be wholly sincere." [109] She had been especially fascinated by the work of Daisetz T. Suzuki, a Japanese Buddhist whose mission was to share his religion and philosophy with the West. When Horney learned that Suzuki was visiting at New York's Columbia University, she invited him to deliver a lecture at the Association for the Advancement of Psychoanalysis. Their friendship shaped the last years of Karen Horney's life.

D. T. Suzuki

Born in Japan in 1870, Teitaro Suzuki's family expected him to enter a profession—law or medicine, like the other men in his family. He chose to study English and found a job as an English teacher, but he felt himself drawn to philosophy and religion as well. He joined a Zen Buddhist monastery in his early twenties. With his facility in languages, Suzuki was soon translating papers on Zen Buddhism from Japanese to English and vice versa. Two formative events happened at about the same time in his life. He agreed to travel to the United States to help translate the great Chinese scripture, the *Tao Te Ching*, the holy book of Taoism, into English. Just before his journey, he achieved enlightenment through his Zen meditation. His master gave him the name of "Daisetsu" (often spelled "Daisetz" in English), which means "Great Simplicity."

Over the years, Suzuki lived in Japan and the United States, Hawaii, and Mexico. His work shifted from translation to authorship, and many go so far as to say that he brought Zen Buddhism to America. He influenced not only Karen Horney and Erich Fromm but also the composer John Cage, the poets Allen Ginsberg and Gary Snyder, and numerous other artists and intellectuals of the twentieth century. He helped Alan Watts write *The Spirit of Zen* in 1936, an early American introduction to the discipline.

Altogether, D. T. Suzuki wrote or contributed to more than thirty books, all dedicated to sharing the philosophy of Zen Buddhism. His book, *An Introduction to Zen Buddhism,* was first published in 1934 and is considered a classic. He was a scholar and a practitioner, a man who knew and appreciated both the East and the West—unusual combinations, that contributed to his genius.

Suzuki invited Karen Horney to join him and several others on a tour of Zen monasteries near Kyoto, Japan. Horney's middle daughter, Brigitte, had recently moved to the United States, and both women were eager to join Suzuki on his trip to the Far East. But politics of the day made it hard for them to do what they wanted.

World War II had ended, leaving many Americans suspicious of both the Germans and the Japanese. Some thought the bigger threat was Communism, though. They suspected anyone in the United States who sympathized with the Russians. They believed that leftist union leaders were plotting to overthrow the American status quo. Some government officials considered it their job to scout out any so-called anti-American elements in the United States. In the early 1950s, they started watching Karen Horney, although they weren't sure if she was a Communist or a Nazi. A postmistress where she had been vacationing had reported suspicions of this woman claiming to be a psychiatrist but sending and receiving volumes of mail from Germany and Mexico. She had ties with the New School for Social Research, which was already blacklisted as a haven of communist sympathizers. It was reported that Horney's books sold well in Russia. Then, an investigator learned how successful Brigitte Horney's acting career had been through the entire Nazi era in Germany, so suspicions turned in that direction. Even J. Edgar Hoover, director of the FBI, wrote a letter identifying Karen Horney as suspicious.

No one had any proof of her connection to anti-American organizations, but the U.S. government certainly wasn't going to renew her passport in order to allow her to visit Japan. Horney staged a campaign, asking for support from friends in high places. She wrote a letter to Dean Acheson, Secretary of State. One friend had connections to the head of the U.S. Passport Division and argued in her favor. Finally her passport was renewed in 1952, more than a year after she requested it, and Karen Horney embarked on a journey to visit Japan and learn about Zen.

All told, Karen Horney spent five weeks in Japan. She traveled with an interesting group of personalities: she and her daughter Brigitte; Suzuki and his American assistant, Richard DeMartino; and a pair of wealthy Americans, long divorced but still friends, both analysis patients of Horney. They were often joined by Akihisa Kondo, a Japanese psychiatrist who was studying the relationship between Western and Asian psychological theories and practice.

They landed in Tokyo, where the devastation of World War II still left the streets in ruins. Kondo had made arrangements for Karen Horney to meet with two of Japan's leading therapists. She also also delivered a talk at the Jikei-kai Medical School, in which she discussed the similarities between her psychoanalytic theories and the theories of Shomo Morita, Japan's predominant psychotherapist. "I was very much impressed by her openness, a dynamic flexibility of mind totally different from the hard, rigid attitude of the orthodox Freudians," said one of the Japanese therapists who met Karen Horney. [110]

From Tokyo, Suzuki led the group to Minokamo, a village about 150 miles west. There they stayed at the Shogenji Temple, a picturesque Zen Buddhist monastery set into the woods. They participated as they could in the daily life of a Zen Buddhist monk—rising before dawn, sitting for meditation, drinking green tea, eating sparsely, observing silence, then joining in on ancient chants. The group did some sightseeing as well, traveling in a fishing boat and visiting Pearl Island to meet the legendary "Pearl King," an aged diver known for his pearl oyster hunting skills.

Karen Horney drank in the landscape and culture of Japan. "I was very much impressed by her tremendous interest in observing and participating in the life of the Japanese people," her traveling companion, Akihisa Kondo, reported later. Richard DeMartino thought she got "a tremendous kick out of it all." [111] It was fun, but it was also inspirational. Kondo sensed that "a strong fermentation process was taking place in her" as she explored the interaction of her own ideas and those of the Japanese traditions. [112]

Only back in the United States did Karen Horney and her friends and family discover that she was struggling with life-threatening cancer. It had started in her gall bladder and was spreading into her lungs. At the insistence of her children, she was admitted into the hospital. She died less than two weeks later.

One of the last conversations Karen Horney had before she died was with a medical student working in the hospital ward where she was staying. "She knew she was dying, and made no effort to conceal her knowledge from me, a stranger," the young man wrote some time later. She asked him how many women were in his class in medical school. *Three women in a total of one hundred students,* he answered. She mused why that should be the case, then talked reflectively about her own life, starting from the time she was a girl, and the decades of struggle it had taken her to gain education, expertise, recognition, and authority. She talked about "the irony that a profession so dedicated to caring for people, nurturing them, . . . should be so overwhelmingly made up of men." Her last words to him were: "You are young, and maybe when you reach my age the world will be quite different." [113] Karen Horney was 67 years old when she died.

THE LEGACY OF KAREN HORNEY

To some degree the hope that Karen Horney expressed on her deathbed has been fulfilled. Between 1970 and 1991, the U.S. government reported, the number of women practicing medicine in the United States quadrupled, from 7.7% of all physicians in 1970 to 30% in 1991. [114] For the first time, in 2003 female medical school applicants outnumbered male in the United States. [115] In the higher ranks of the medical and the psychiatric professions, however, the proportion of women is still low. [116]

As a pioneering woman seeking to be a leader in medicine and psychiatry, Karen Horney was ahead of her times. There are other ways in which she and her ideas were prophetic. Few psychiatrists today strictly follow the traditional methods of Freudian psychoanalysis. Most now believe, as Karen Horney stated to the shock of so many, that Freudian theories are useful but not necessarily the only ways to understand personality or manage therapy. Many woman have come forward with critiques founded on the arguments of Karen Horney, echoing her point that Freud's view of human psychology was male-centered and inaccurate, especially in its picture of the psychology of women. Not only the ideas but also the techniques of psychotherapy have evolved significantly in the half-century since Karen Horney's death, and in many ways the ideas that she dared to voice now seem commonplace, obvious, and second-nature. In her day, though, those ideas were radical, inventive, new, and brilliant. No matter how difficult, self-centered, or stubborn she was, everyone admired her for daring to discover, then to be, herself.

Chronology

1885 Born on September 15 near Hamburg, Germany

1901 Enrolled in Gymnasium

1904 Moved with mother and brother into city of Hamburg

1906 Entered medical school at University of Freiburg

1906 Met Oskar Horney

1908 Graduated from medical school, moved to Göttingen for residency

Timeline

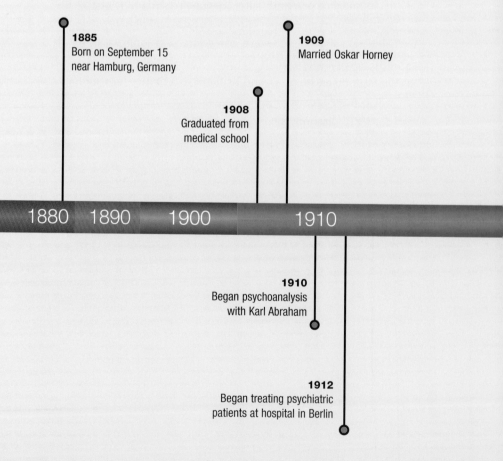

1885
Born on September 15
near Hamburg, Germany

1909
Married Oskar Horney

1908
Graduated from
medical school

1880   1890   1900   1910

1910
Began psychoanalysis
with Karl Abraham

1912
Began treating psychiatric
patients at hospital in Berlin

1909	Married Oskar Horney, moved to Berlin
1910	Wackels Danielsen, her father, died
1910	Began psychoanalysis with Karl Abraham
1911	Sonni Danielsen, her mother, died
1911	Brigitte Horney, her first daughter, born
1912	Began treating psychiatric patients at hospital in Berlin

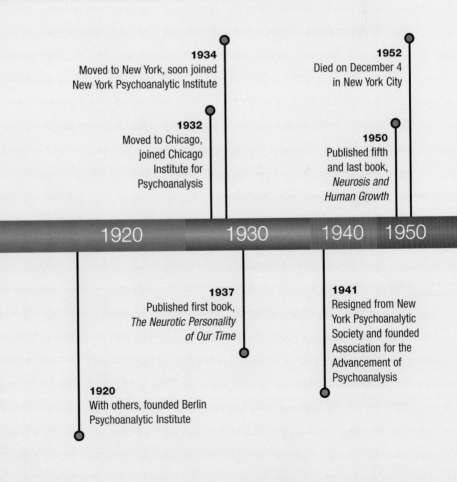

1934
Moved to New York, soon joined
New York Psychoanalytic Institute

1952
Died on December 4
in New York City

1932
Moved to Chicago,
joined Chicago
Institute for
Psychoanalysis

1950
Published fifth
and last book,
*Neurosis and
Human Growth*

1920   1930   1940   1950

1937
Published first book,
*The Neurotic Personality
of Our Time*

1941
Resigned from New
York Psychoanalytic
Society and founded
Association for the
Advancement of
Psychoanalysis

1920
With others, founded Berlin
Psychoanalytic Institute

Chronology

1913	Marianne Horney, her second daughter, born
1916	Renate Horney, her third daughter, born
1917	Delivered lecture, "The Technique of Psychoanalytic Therapy"
1920	With others, founded Berlin Psychoanalytic Institute
1923	Stinnes Corporation, Oskar Horney's employer, failed
1926	Contributed "The Flight from Womanhood" to Freud *Festschrift*
1927	Separated from Oskar Horney
1932	Moved with daughter Renate to Chicago, joined Chicago Institute for Psychoanalysis
1934	Moved to New York, associated with New York Psychoanalytic Institute
1935	Began teaching at New School for Social Research
1935	Became member of New York Psychoanalytic Institute
1937	Published first book, *The Neurotic Personality of Our Time*
1939	Published second book, *New Goals in Psychoanalysis*
1941	Demoted at New York Psychoanalytic Institute
1941	With four others, resigned from New York Psychoanalytic Society
1941	Founded Association for the Advancement of Psychoanalysis
1942	Published third book, *Self-Analysis*
1945	Published fourth book, *Our Inner Conflicts*
1950	Published last book, *Neurosis and Human Growth*
1952	Traveled in Japan for five weeks, learning about Zen Buddhism
1952	Died on December 4 in New York City

Analysis—The tracing of unconscious motivations to their source.

Analyst—One who is licensed to practice psychoanalysis; psychoanalyst.

Anthropology—The study of the origins and social relationships of humans.

Anti-Semitism—Prejudice against Jewish people.

Aryan—In Nazi Germany, applied to inhabitants of non-Jewish extraction.

Castration complex—In males, the fear of castration; in females, the belief that it has already happened.

Collective unconscious—The deeper, spiritual level of the unconscious that reflects experiences common to all human beings.

Compulsive behaviors—Unconscious actions that people perform, often repetitively, in order to avoid ideas or desires that arouse anxiety.

Cultural studies—The study of shared beliefs, values, customs, behaviors, and artifacts.

Culture—The system of shared beliefs, values, customs, behaviors, and artifacts that members of society share.

Ego—The central sense of self, the conscious self-image a person carries, and the part of the person that mediates between the id and the real world.

Émigrés—People who had fled one country (such as Nazi Germany) to settle in another (such as the United States).

Evolutionary—Guided by processes of growth, change, and development.

Free association—A psychotherapy technique in which the patient is encouraged to talk freely and let words and ideas flow without reflection or self-control.

Gestalt therapy—A present-centered approach to analysis that focuses on the here-and-now rather than the past.

Gymnasium—The German equivalent of high school.

Glossary

Hypnosis—A technique in which a sleeplike state induced by suggestion is used to develop therapeutic insights and self-awareness.

Id—The most primitive part of an individual; the urges and needs at the core of being.

Instincts—The impulses that drive actions.

Mechanistic—Running like a machine; operating strictly according to cause and effect.

Medical residency—Postgraduate medical training and practice.

Neuroses—Psychological abnormalities caused by unresolved conflicts.

Oedipus complex—Attachment of the child to the parent of the opposite sex, accompanied by envious and aggressive feelings toward the parent of the same sex.

Orthodox Freudians—Those who strictly follow Freud's theories.

Penis envy—The notion that females envy male characteristics, especially the possession of a penis.

Psychiatrist—One who practices psychiatry.

Psychiatry—The branch of medicine dealing with the diagnosis and treatment of mental and psychological illnesses.

Psychoanalysis—Developed initially by Freud, a set of techniques for exploring underlying motives and a method of treating various mental disorders.

Psychoanalyst—One who is licensed to practice psychoanalysis; analyst.

Psychology—The scientific study of human behavior and the functioning of the mind.

Psychologist—One who practices psychology. Unlike a psychiatrist, a psychologist does not have a medical degree.

Psychic—Pertaining to the human psyche.

Psyche—The mind as the center of thought, emotion, and behavior.

Social sciences—Disciplines that study the relationship of the individual with society, including anthropology, economics, and sociology.

Sociology—The study of human societies.

Sublimation—Diverting the expression of instincts into productive, more acceptable uses.

Superego—The individual's conscience, aware of laws, rules, and other people's expectations.

Therapy—The treatment of mental or emotional problems based on analysis.

Transference—A technique in which the patient is encouraged to play out and then explore his or her troubled personal relationships by mirroring them in interactions with the therapist.

Unconscious—The still active, although unrecognized, forces of the mind that are not ordinarily available to conscious awareness.

Zen Buddhism—A discipline asserting that enlightenment can come through meditation and self-awareness rather than faith.

Notes

Chapter 1

1. Karen Horney, *New Ways in Psychoanalysis* (New York: W. W. Norton & Co., 1939), p. 18.

2. Ibid., p. 21.

3. Ibid., p. 36.

4. Ibid., p. 46.

5. Ibid., p. 282.

6. Ibid., p. 282.

7. Ibid., p. 305.

8. Bernard Paris, *Karen Horney: A Psychoanalyst's Search for Self-Understanding* (New Haven and London: Yale University Press, 1994), p. 151.

9. Susan Quinn, *A Mind of Her Own: The Life of Karen Horney* (New York: Summit Books, 1977), p. 333.

10. Ibid.

11. Horney, *New Ways*, p. 133.

12. Ibid., p. 42.

13. Ibid.

14. Ibid., p. 152.

15. Ibid.

16. Ibid., pp. 152-153.

17. Quoted in Quinn, *A Mind of Her Own*, p. 334.

18. Jack L. Rubins, *Karen Horney: Gentle Rebel of Psychoanalysis* (New York: Dial Press, 1978), p. 235.

Chapter 2

19. As quoted in Quinn, *A Mind of Her Own*, p. 48.

20. *The Adolescent Diaries of Karen Horney* (New York: Basic Books, 1980), p. 11.

21. Ibid., 20.

22. Ibid., p. 19.

23. Ibid.

24. Ibid., p. 88.

25. Ibid., p. 67.

26. Ibid., p. 68.

27. Ibid., p. 69.

28. Ibid., p. 70.

29. Ibid., pp. 148-149.

30. Ibid., p. 102.

31. As quoted in Quinn, *A Mind of Her Own*, p. 127.

32. *Adolescent Diaries*, p. 148.

33. As quoted in Quinn, *A Mind of Her Own*, p. 113.

Chapter 3

34. *Adolescent Diaries*, pp. 240, 242.

35. As reported in Quinn, *A Mind of Her Own*, p. 180.

36. As quoted in Quinn, *A Mind of Her Own*, p. 148.

37. As quoted in Quinn, *A Mind of Her Own*, p. 149.

38. Quoted in Harold Kelman, M.D., Introduction, in Karen Horney, *Feminine Psychology* (New York: W. W. Norton & Co., 1967), p. 13.

39. As quoted in Quinn, *A Mind of Her Own*, p. 197.

40. As quoted in Quinn, *A Mind of Her Own*, p. 200.

41. Ibid.

42. Sigmund Freud, "Woman as Castrated Man," in Rosemary Agonito, *History of Ideas on Woman: A Source Book* (New York: G. P. Putnam's Sons, 1977), pp. 311-313.

43. Karen Horney, "Genesis of Castration Complex," in *Feminine Psychology*, p. 38.

44. Karen Horney, "The Flight from Womanhood," in *Feminine Psychology*, p. 54.

45. Ibid., p. 55.

46. Ibid., pp. 57, 59.

47. Ibid., p. 60.

48. Ibid., pp. 69, 70.

49. Ibid., p. 70.

50. As quoted in Kelman, Introduction, *Feminine Psychology*, p. 25.

Chapter 4

51. As quoted in Quinn, *A Mind of Her Own*, p. 247.

52. As quoted in Quinn, *A Mind of Her Own*, p. 252.

53. Horney, "The Overvaluation of Love," in *Feminine Psychology*, p. 183.

54. Ibid., p. 212.

55. Horney, *New Ways in Psychoanalysis*, p. 12.

56. As quoted in Quinn, *A Mind of Her Own*, p. 274.

57. Ibid., p. 277.

58. Ibid., p. 282.

59. Ibid., p. 285.

Chapter 5

60. As quoted in Rubins, *Karen Horney: Gentle Rebel*, p. 202.

61. As quoted in Quinn, *A Mind of Her Own*, p. 291.

62. Ibid., p. 293.

63. As quoted in Rubins, *Karen Horney: Gentle Rebel*, p. 204.

64. As quoted in Quinn, *A Mind of Her Own*, p. 296.

65. Ibid., p. 308.

66. Horney, *The Neurotic Personality of Our Time*, pp. vii-viii.

67. Ibid., p. viii.

68. Ibid.

69. Ibid.

70. Ibid., p. ix.

71. Ibid.

72. Horney, *Neurotic Personality*, p. 80.

73. As quoted in Quinn, *A Mind of Her Own*, p. 368.

74. Ibid., p. 306.

75. Ibid., p. 309.

76. Ibid.

77. Ibid., p. 310.

78. As quoted in Rubins, *Karen Horney: Gentle Rebel*, p. 210.

79. As quoted in Quinn, *A Mind of Her Own*, p. 311.

Chapter 6

80. As quoted in Quinn, *A Mind of Her Own*, p. 336.

81. As quoted in Rubins, *Karen Horney: Gentle Rebel*, p. 238.

82. As quoted in Quinn, *A Mind of Her Own*, pp. 338-339.

83. Ibid., p. 344.

84. Ibid.

85. Ibid., p. 346.

86. Ibid., p. 347.

87. Ibid.

88. Ibid.

Notes

89. Ibid., p. 345.

90. Ibid., p. 348.

91. As quoted in Rubins, *Karen Horney: Gentle Rebel*, p. 240.

Chapter 7

92. As quoted in Quinn, *A Mind of Her Own*, p. 353.

93. Karen Horney, *Self-Analysis* (New York: W. W. Norton & Co., 1942), p. 7.

94. Ibid., p. 8.

95. As quoted in Quinn, *A Mind of Her Own*, p. 356.

96. Horney, *Self-Analysis*, p. 40.

97. Ibid., p. 48-49.

98. As quoted in Quinn, *A Mind of Her Own*, p. 354-355.

99. Ibid., pp. 357-358.

100. Ibid., p. 360.

101. Quinn, *A Mind of Her Own*, p. 361.

102. As quoted in Quinn, *A Mind of Her Own*, p. 381.

103. Ibid., p. 383.

104. Karen Horney, *Our Inner Conflicts* (New York: W. W. Norton & Co., 1945), p. 15.

105. Ibid., p. 241.

106. As quoted in Quinn, *A Mind of Her Own*, p. 387.

107. Karen Horney, *Neurosis and Human Growth* (New York: W. W. Norton & Co., 1950), p. 15.

108. As quoted in Quinn, *A Mind of Her Own*, p. 388.

108. Horney, *Our Inner Conflicts*, pp. 162-163.

110. As quoted in Quinn, *A Mind of Her Own*, p. 408.

111. Ibid., p. 411.

112. Ibid., p. 414.

113. Ibid., p. 417.

114. Council on Graduate Medical Education, *Women in Medicine*, Fifth Report, May 1998, [http://www.cogme.gov/rpt5.htm].

115. Association of American Medical Colleges, Press Release, "Applicants to U.S. Medical Schools Increase, Women the Majority for the First Time," Washington, D.C., November 4, 2003.

116. As reported in C. D. De Angelis, "Women in Academic Medicine: New Insights, Same Sad News," *New England Journal of Medicine*, vol. 342, no. 6 (February 10, 2000); and in L. W. Reiser et al., "Beginning careers in academic psychiatry for women— "Bermuda Triangle"?, *American Journal of Psychiatry*, vol. 150 (1993), 1392-1397.

Agonito, Rosemary, *History of Ideas on Woman: A Source Book* (New York: G. P. Putnam's Sons, 1977).

De Angelis, C. D., "Women in Academic Medicine: New Insights, Same Sad News," *New England Journal of Medicine,* vol. 342, no. 6 (February 10, 2000).

Fromm, Erich, *Escape from Freedom* (New York: Farrar & Rinehart, 1941).

Horney, Karen, *The Adolescent Diaries of Karen Horney* (New York: Basic Books, 1980).

Horney, Karen, *Feminine Psychology* (New York: W. W. Norton & Co., 1967).

Horney, Karen, *Neurosis and Human Growth* (New York: W. W. Norton & Co., 1950).

Horney, Karen, *New Ways in Psychoanalysis* (New York: W. W. Norton & Co., 1939).

Horney, Karen, *Our Inner Conflicts* (New York: W. W. Norton & Co., 1945).

Horney, Karen , *Self-Analysis* (New York: W. W. Norton & Co., 1942).

Paris, Bernard, *Karen Horney: A Psychoanalyst's Search for Self-Understanding* (New Haven and London: Yale University Press, 1994).

Quinn, Susan, *A Mind of Her Own: The Life of Karen Horney* (New York: Summit Books, 1977).

L. W. Reiser et al., "Beginning careers in academic psychiatry for women—"Bermuda Triangle"?, *American Journal of Psychiatry,* vol. 150 (1993), 1392-1397.

Rubins, Jack L., *Karen Horney: Gentle Rebel of Psychoanalysis* (New York: Dial Press, 1978).

WEB SOURCES:

Council on Graduate Medical Education, *Women in Medicine,* Fifth Report, May 1998, http://www.cogme.gov/rpt5.htm

Rainer Funk, "Erich Fromm's Life and Work," website of the International Erich Fromm Society, http://www.erichfromm.de/english/life/life_bio2.html

Further Reading

Freud, Sigmund, *On Dreams* (New York: W. W. Norton & Co., 1990).

Fromm, Erich, *The Art of Loving* (New York: Harper & Row, 1974).

Kahn, Michael, *Basic Freud: Psychoanalytic Thought for the 21st Century* (New York: Basic Books, 2002).

Mitchell, Stephen A., and Margaret J. Black, *Freud and Beyond: A History of Modern Psychoanalytic Thought* (New York: Basic Books, 1996).

Muckenhoupt, Margaret, *Sigmund Freud: Explorer of the Unconscious* (New York: Oxford University Press, 1991).

Reef, Catherine, *Sigmund Freud: Pioneer of the Mind* (New York: Clarion Books, 2001).

Sayers, Janet, *Mothers of Psychoanalysis: Helene Deutsch, Karen Horney, Anna Freud, Melanie Klein* (New York: W. W. Norton & Co., 1991).

WEBSITES

"Freud, Conflict, & Culture," Library of Congress Exhibition
http://lcweb.loc.gov/exhibits/freud/

International Karen Horney Society
http://plaza.ufl.edu/bjparis/

Association for the Advancement of Psychoanalysis
and Karen Horney Psychoanalytic Center
http://www.karenhorneycenter.org

Index

Index

Index

About the Author

Susan Tyler Hitchcock's books include *Gather Ye Wild Things: A Forager's Year; Coming About: A Family Passage at Sea; The University of Virginia: A Pictorial History;* and *Mad Mary Lamb: Lunacy and Murder in Literary London,* to be published by W. W. Norton & Co. in 2005. She holds a B.A. and M.A. in English from the University of Michigan and a Ph.D. in English from the University of Virginia. She and her husband have two children and live near Charlottesville, Virginia.